This book is dedicated to Sarah MacDougall,
for showing me her artist's heart.
She reminds me every day of why.

REBENT SINNER

REBENT SINNER
IVAN COYOTE

ARSENAL PULP PRESS
VANCOUVER

REBENT SINNER

ARSENAL PULP PRESS
Suite 202 – 211 East Georgia St.
Vancouver, BC V6A 1Z6
Canada
arsenalpulp.com

The publisher gratefully acknowledges the support of the Canada Council for the Arts and the British Columbia Arts Council for its publishing program, and the Government of Canada, and the Government of British Columbia (through the Book Publishing Tax Credit Program), for its publishing activities.

Arsenal Pulp Press acknowledges the xʷməθkʷəy̓əm (Musqueam), Sḵwx̱wú7mesh (Squamish), and səl̓ilwətaʔɬ (Tsleil-Waututh) Nations, speakers of Hul'q'umi'num'/Halq'eméylem/hən̓q̓əmin̓əm̓ and custodians of the traditional, ancestral, and unceded territories where our office is located. We pay respect to their histories, traditions, and continuous living cultures and commit to accountability, respectful relations, and friendship.

Cover and text design by Oliver McPartlin
Cover artwork by Christine Fellows
Edited by Shirarose Wilensky
Proofread by [tk]

Printed and bound in Canada

Library and Archives Canada Cataloguing in Publication:
Title: Rebent sinner / Ivan Coyote.
Names: Coyote, Ivan E. (Ivan Elizabeth), 1969- author.
Identifiers: Canadiana (print) 20190123958 | Canadiana (ebook) 20190123966 | ISBN 9781551527734
   (softcover) | ISBN 9781551527741 (HTML)
Subjects: LCSH: Coyote, Ivan E. (Ivan Elizabeth), 1969- | LCSH: Transgender people—Identity. |
   LCSH: Gender-nonconforming people. | LCSH: Transgender people—Canada—Biography. | LCSH:
   Gender-nonconforming people—Canada—Biography.
Classification: LCC HQ77.8 C69 2019 | DDC 306.768092—dc23

CONTENTS

1. Blood.. 9

2. Here 25

3. Market 33

4. Street.. 43

5. There.. 51

6. Rebent Sinner... 77

7. Show and Tell 99

8. Class...111

9. The Last Time I Saw Richard 123

10. To and From..181

11. Chest 209

1. BLOOD

My gran used to smoke the cheap cigarettes. John Player Specials, Craven A menthols, Number 7s. She'd buy them by the carton and squirrel them away in the closet in her bedroom.

My uncles would swipe one from her open pack on the kitchen table, and cough and stare down at the red cherry between their fingertips and say, "Fuck, Mum. These are awful. Why can't you get Du Mauriers? Export As?" She would make that noise with her tongue and tuck the rest of the pack into her purse.

She had one of those little cigarette machines, too, where you buy the filters and tubes and the tobacco in a tin, and she and my aunts would sit around the table and stuff little wads of tobacco into the groove in the machine and slide it back and forth, and a cigarette would pop out the end. You had to get the perfect amount of tobacco in there to get it to burn just right, "But look how much cheaper it is," they would all say, like they were trying to convince each other of something none of them truly believed.

My gran unknowingly smoked her last cigarette on a Friday afternoon, and she broke her hip that night, when her foot fell off the footstool during *Jeopardy!* and her heel hit the floor at a weird angle. She always said that new hardwood floor was easier to sweep than the carpet ever was to keep vacuumed. She was hospitalized right away, went into a coma, and died the following Wednesday without ever really waking up again. She was almost ninety years old. It all happened so fast, but hey, "At least she never had to quit smoking," everybody said.

Dear favourite uncle: I'm going to have to insist you stop using my deadname. I changed it in 1993. That was ... more than twenty-five years ago. I'm afraid "I just can't get used to it" is no longer an acceptable excuse. Lesser uncles are gaining on you. I still love you, but collect yourself.

I'M COMING HOME in fifteen days. I will come and see you in the new place. I look like your sons did when they were my age. I look like your grandson, and his son looks like me. You might be confused, but I know you will recognize the blood in me. Your blood in me. I will touch your supersoft hands and marvel at all those blue maps on the backs of them.

"What should I get you for your ninety-seventh birthday?" I will ask you.

"What?" you will say.

"Your birthday," I will repeat louder.

"My what?" you will say. "Oh, that. I'm good. I have everything I need right here. These people, they take good care of me," you will say.

LAST MONTH I was home in the Yukon and I went to visit my ninety-seven-year-old grandmother in the nursing home where she has been for the last year, since her accident. It had been a few months since I had seen her. It was about eight p.m., dark and cold outside. The heat was cranked up inside the nursing home. I was sweating in my unzipped parka as I walked down the maze of hallways, through the dining hall, and into her room. She was asleep, and my heart twisted in my chest at the sight of her: asleep on her side in her hospital bed, her nightdress pulled up to reveal her unbearably thin and bruised legs, and her diaper.

She woke up as I sat in the rolling chair next to her bed. "It's you!" she cried out, with joy and surprise. "Look at you! My beautiful boy!"

She sat up and patted the mattress beside her withered thighs, pulled her nightdress down a little, but not all the way. I sat beside her. The plastic sheet on the mattress crinkled under us both.

"My beautiful, beautiful boy. You're so handsome. You've always been so handsome. I'm so glad you are here."

She reached out a pencil-like arm and pulled my head down to what was left of her once ample chest. She stroked my head and cupped my cheek. She was never very physically affectionate before, but she's changing, my uncle Rob had warned me on the phone months ago. "She's slipping a little mentally, too," he had said. "She is getting confused easily, not recognizing people some days. Don't take it personally if she thinks you're one of the staff or something," he told me.

Does she think I'm Rob, or my dad, or one of her other sons? I wondered, and hugged her back. She felt like she was made of bird bones and tissue paper.

"My beautiful, beautiful boy," she cooed over and over. Then she looked me right in both eyes, her papery palm still cradling my cheek. "Is that what I should call you? Do I call you my beautiful grandson, or my granddaughter? I never know with you."

In late May 2017, my uncle Rob went to visit his mom, my grand-mother, Patricia. She asked him what day it was.

"It's Saturday," he told her.

She took a small breath and announced it was going to be her last Saturday on this earth.

"You don't know that, Mom," Rob said, but she gave him that look. Her look. She had a real withering look she could lay on you— it was kind of terrifying—and she remained capable of wielding it far longer than she should have physically been able to. It was usually paired with a frustrated blast of nose breath, exhaled over pursed lips.

"This is my last Saturday," she repeated. "I feel a ... new kind of tired coming over me. There's a girl that works here, her name is Crystal. She only works weekends, but she's not here today because she's in Las Vegas with her sisters, so I won't see her again. Please tell her how much I enjoyed our little chats. Tell her that she is really good at her job, but she should keep up with her studies. Tell her to stay in school. And I need you to do me one last thing."

Rob nodded.

"I need you to go and get me a few things. I need"—and if I know her, she counted them off on her left hand with the first slender finger of her right—"four cards, four envelopes, four blank cheques, my exact bank balance, and a pen." She shot him that look again. "A good pen."

So, ever the dutiful son, Rob went downtown and got everything and came back about an hour later. He pulled the little rolling table over and she half sat up in her hospital bed. She divided her remaining money into four exactly equal sums and wrote four cheques, one for each of her four sons. She tucked each cheque into an envelope and told Rob to make sure they all cashed them right away. "Don't wait, even a day. Don't let the bank swallow up even a penny of this in their red tape." She was adamant about this.

Then she opened up the first card and wrote: *Dear Robert. You were always my favourite son. Don't tell your brothers.* In the second card she wrote: *Dear Donald. You were always my favourite son. Don't tell your brothers.* Then, *Dear Fred. You were always my favourite son* ... and so on.

I was in a hotel in Melbourne, Australia, when I got the call. It was the middle of the night. It was my mom. I knew from the sound of her breathing, before she even said a word.

"I'm so sorry to wake you," she said. "She had a stroke on Sunday morning and never really woke up again. We didn't call you because we knew you wouldn't make it home anyway, and you two had such a good visit in February. Your uncle Rob wanted me to be sure to tell you she was herself, right up until the very end."

ABSENCE MAKES THE smart grow harder.

Absence makes the heart go longer.

My dog Chippy was nearly eighteen when he died. It was three years ago this past March 1, 2019. His real name was Goliath, but I never called him that. I named him before I knew him, I guess. He was so little I thought he needed a big name, but he didn't. He wasn't small and mighty; he was tiny and deep. When I think back on our many years together (he was seven weeks old, I think, when we first met), I think I loved our last few years together the most. Sure, it was great when he was young and could climb mountains and still want to go for a walk when we got home. But I learned to cherish those slow, slow, slow totters around the same block in the last few years even more. How he would still make a little helping jump whenever I picked him up. How he would find the little dips in the curb when his bones got too old to step down too far. I recorded his snores, and I still have them on my phone, videos too. I will probably listen to them after I finish typing this.

He taught me so much in those last years: how to slow down and be patient, how to nurture and take care in a different way, how to love him through shit and blood and watery eyes and midnight meds. How to love him still when he forgot who I even was some days, in the end. How to not leave the chairs pulled away from the table after he went blind. I will never forget any of those last years, and I cherish all of them. Falling asleep listening to his wheezy snoring. Waking up and listening for him to still be breathing.

IT IS THE morning of June 13, 2016. The day after a twenty-nine-year-old security guard killed forty-nine people and wounded fifty-three others in a mass shooting inside Pulse, a gay dance club in Orlando, Florida.

I talked to my dad today. It's been a while. He's been sick, with a fairly serious condition, and his dog broke his leg, and it cost him a lot of dough. He's nearly seventy and still working a physically hard job, welding heavy equipment. He's alone, even in my big family, partly because he can be mean and he pushes people away. I don't think he means to, but he does. We talked about all of this, even the hard stuff. That's the thing about him and me. We've always been able to talk. It wasn't perfect, that conversation, but neither is either of us.

We talked about Orlando. He must have seen it on the TV news. He brought it up, asked me how I was doing.

I told him I was hurting, that everyone I knew was hurting. He said even though he only knows a bunch of redneck old Yukoners, none of them cares if anyone is gay anymore. He said, "It's getting better, isn't it? I mean, aside from shit like this, isn't it getting better?"

I said, "Yeah, maybe so, Dad. Maybe it's getting better some days, but they are still passing laws to keep us out of bathrooms, they are still passing laws to make it okay to fire us, or to not sell us a fucking wedding cake." And I said I figured that was part of the shit that creates the hate that twists a man's head enough that he could go in there and do something like that. I said, "Dad, did you know that queer people lined up to donate blood yesterday in Orlando, Florida? They lined up down the block to give blood, and they wouldn't take it."

He started to cry. Then I started to cry.

I wasn't even going to call him today because I've been so mad at him. But I'm glad I did.

I'M GOING TO miss having the writer Richard Wagamese in the world with us. I really am. His death gutted me in a very visceral way, so hard that I knew right away it wasn't just because we were both heart storytellers, not just because we looked each other right in the eye bones every time our paths crossed and just saw. Richard's death rattled me because of my own father. Because even though I still don't know how Richard died, I know it was because of booze and pain and the past always there, rapping and banging on a man from inside.

When I heard, my heart crumpled because if handsome, talented Richard, with his enormous heart full of stories, with his good teeth and always the best shirts and so much wisdom and generosity and awards and books and accolades couldn't outrun it, how will my father? My father, with his bent back and burning eyes and shaking hands, still welding greasy, filthy equipment in the cold in the Yukon at seventy-something years old and going to bed not wanting to get up—how's he ever going to make it?

Well, it's not perfect, but he's making it today. He's going to a meeting today. He says he hates telling the same story over and over, but the people are okay. They're all just drunks like him, with awful stories too, he says, but he does feel better after.

YESTERDAY I MET a painter. He is seventy-eight, a distant cousin of my partner Sarah's, and he lives in a little Swedish fishing village. He has lived in the same house for thirty-eight years, and painted pictures of his village and the harbour there for all thirty-eight of those years. I fell in love with one particular painting, of the piers and the ocean and two little boats.

"Ah, that one." He pointed from where he was sitting on a little chair next to the door of his gallery. "I had a health problem not too long ago. I had too much blood pressure here, in my head. They had to operate and put a thing in my head, a little ..." He searches for the English word for it. "A valve? It goes down here ..." He makes us both touch a lump, a tube, that now lives under his thin silver tuft of hair and his tender scalp. "It very much affected my balance, this condition, and for some time, I lost the ability to paint at all. While I was healing, I would lie on the beach and study the clouds. I began to understand them better, then, their characters and how they behave. I would watch them all day. When I began to be able to paint again, I included more sky. The sky is now bigger to me in my paintings. This one, the one you noticed, it was the first one I finished after I learned more about the sky."

He touched my face when we said goodbye.

Sarah bought that little painting. I could not stop looking at it, propped up on a chair in the corner of the room. I knew it contained a magic story that I would remember and return to whenever the pressure in my head started to affect the balance of my life.

TORSTEN ERASMIE, SARAH'S cousin the painter, died ten days later, on a Sunday afternoon. His daughter had come to visit the day before.

That little painting of two boats and the piers in his harbour now hangs on the wall in Sarah's living room, right next to a needlepoint piece that her grandmother Kitty made depicting a bouquet of blue flowers.

I now think of him every time I slow down enough to take notice of which way the clouds are moving. I now remember to include more sky.

2. HERE

IT IS GREAT to be home. I am really tired. Sometimes, keeping the butch-in-an-unfamiliar-small-town protective force field activated for six days in a row can take it out of you.

I GOT INTO the elevator with the small dog, and a little boy and his mom. The boy was visibly scared of the dog, so I made Chippy sit beside my feet, away from the boy and his mom.

"Why is that dog shaking?" the boy asked.

"He is scared of you," I told the boy. Chippy sometimes quivered in elevators; he didn't like them.

"Why is he scared of me?" the boy asked, a little chuffed at the thought.

"Because you are so big and strong," I told him.

"But I am only four," he responded.

"But look how little the dog is, and how big you must look to him," I said.

The boy immediately squatted right in front of the dog, bending in that way that only kids can bend so his nose was nearly touching Chippy's. "Don't be afraid of me, and I won't be afraid of you," he said.

Then the elevator dinged at their floor and his mom grabbed his hand to walk him out. He looked over his shoulder and smiled and said, "Tell that dog I am only a little boy."

As I write this in 2017, Trump is about to embarrass us all as he embarks on his first tour abroad, and his international hosts have been prepped to make sure he gets well- done steak with a side of ketchup alongside the traditional local cuisine. Everyone was warned that he prefers short speeches with lots of visual aids. The president of the United States of America doesn't like to listen much to anyone else, or read anything.

Back in Canada, our senate is still undecided about whether trans people should be afforded basic human rights under our charter of rights and freedoms. One of the witnesses the senate called to testify is a tenured professor and a virulent transphobe who claims that being asked to refer to his students by their proper pronouns is a violation of his right to free speech, and my own government just paid for his airfare and hotel to facilitate them listening to his bigotry.

We have climate change and North Korean nukes and child poverty.

And I can't even move to Canada because I already live in Canada.

So what do I do to get through it all?

I punch Nazis in the face every time I get a chance.

Just kidding. I'm not the punching type.

Instead, whenever I get home from the road, I cook. Nothing fancy. Comfort food: stews, shepherd's pie, potato salad, red curry, roast chicken. Then I make chicken soup with the bones. Like, really good chicken soup. I eat some and freeze the rest. I deliver it to friends with new babies or head colds or deadlines or final exams or breast cancer. A fairly wide selection of East Vancouver residents owe me my Tupperware back. "Shut up and show up," my grandma Pat once said to me after her neighbour's husband died and she was making her a pot of macaroni and cheese. "That's what your great-grandmother Monica used to say during the Depression."

Clean sheets.

Clean towels.

Clean clothes.

Clean house. I bleach stuff and scrub floors and take a toothbrush to the grout between the tiles in the bathroom. Pine cleaner and orange cleaner and stainless-steel polish and special stuff for the granite countertops. It might be a gimmick, but fuck it, I don't even care.

Then there is my garden. I'm a condo dweller, so I don't have access to any actual dirt in the ground, but I have two small balconies. I prune and cajole and water and pluck and weed and fertilize and spray and smell. My bleeding heart flowered like you wouldn't believe this spring, and yes, I do think it's a metaphor, and yes, I take it as a sign.

I talk to strangers in my neighbourhood. Neighbours and shop-keepers and delivery guys and the mail person and panhandlers and buskers and the ladies working the parking lot of the 7-Eleven up the street from my building. I listen to them. I learn their names. I learn the names of their spouses and kids and cats and dogs. I've done it for many years now, so there are now fewer real strangers in my neighbourhood.

I used to walk my old dog. My old deaf and blind and quaking dog. Two or three times a day for seventeen years, until March 1, 2016, a year and a bit ago. Now I walk my puppy. He's seven months old and his name is Lucky. We named him after me.

I play the guitar and the ukulele. I'm currently learning all the hits of my misspent youth in the seventies and eighties. I do really killer versions of "Time after Time" by Cyndi Lauper and "Do You Really Want to Hurt Me" by Culture Club.

After I get home from the road, I see how long I can go without putting on pants.

I lift weights. I've been going to the same gym for twenty-seven years now. One time, a woman who had just moved to the neighbourhood went up to the front desk to tell them that there was a man in the women's change room.

"Oh, that's just Ivan," the staff member told her. "Ivan's been coming here longer than any of us have worked here. Ivan has outlasted the last three, maybe four, owners. If you've got a problem with that, there are yoga classes at Good Life Fitness up the street. Would you like the address?"

I have dinner parties. Very big, very delicious gluten-free dinner parties. There are always leftovers.

I listen to records and drink really good coffee and smoke weed on the balcony. I drink bourbon, but only the good stuff. I don't really believe there is such a thing as bad bourbon.

I do cross-stitch and collect neckties.

And if none of that works, I punch Nazis in the face.

I COOK MY way all through the dark part of the year. I burn candles and hang lights, and I decorate a live tree for solstice. I have pine and cedar incense that smells like a campfire from back home. I wash the sheets at least once a week and put lots of blankets on the bed so the covers are heavy on me. I spend time under the moon on purpose when it's clear. Stargazing.

3. MARKET

THIS JUST HAPPENED at the grocery store: a woman in her eighties left her headlights on in her car. I locked my groceries in my truck and followed her back into the store. She was at the till already, cashing in a lottery ticket. I told her that she had left her headlights on, and she thanked me profusely.

As I was walking away she said to the young cashier, "Now that is what we need more of, nice gentlemen like that."

The cashier said, "I don't think she was a gentleman."

The old woman shook her head hard and insisted, "I am old enough to know a gentleman when I see one. You should go out and find yourself one like that."

The cashier smiled at me and said, "Okay, then, maybe I will."

I GO INTO my local record store looking for a Larkin Poe album. It's not on the shelves, so I ask the woman working there if she can order it for me. It's just her and me, and an older, bearded, pretty straight-looking rock dude in a Metallica T-shirt, in the store. The woman looks pretty queer to me. You can't assume anything, but I'm pretty sure she's family.

She looks up the band—a two-woman group—on the computer. "Are they sisters?" she asks me.

"I think so," I tell her.

"Because they have the same last name," she continues, tapping on the keyboard.

Metallica T-shirt dude freezes and looks up at both of us. "Or they could be married, you know. You should think about that, before you assume anything." He seems pretty indignant about it all, even a little miffed. He leaves without buying anything.

The woman and I crack up a little.

"Did he just chastise us for being heterosexist?" I ask her.

"I think that's what just happened." She laughs.

"I think that was my favourite part of this day so far," I tell her.

"Best part of my day, for sure," she says. "And if we don't call you in two weeks it means we couldn't find your record."

SEMI-DRUNK AND DEFINITELY creepy dude in the lineup at the market says to uninterested young mother: "Is that a new baby?"

Young mom retorts coolly: "Is there such a thing as an old baby?"

Even the clerk laughed.

There is a kid singing "I want to wish you a dairy Christmas" at the top of her lungs to her mom in front of the milk and cheese coolers at the market right now and it's really cracking me up.

KID AT THE grocery store: "I don't want vegetables. You don't give me what I want. You are a bad daddy."

Dad: "Bad daddy? I like the sound of that."

And right there, all of a sudden, he got magically way better looking to me.

ME TO A guy wearing a baby in a carrier standing next to me in the supermarket lineup: "If you had a half-chewed piece of cracker stuck to the side of your head, would you want someone to tell you?"

Guy with the baby, with resignation: "Probably not."

"Well, then," I say, "forget I said anything."

I SAW "MAN candles" in a store the other day. They smelled like misogyny and unshed tears. Just kidding. They smelled like cedar and smoke, but I would never buy them.

4. STREET

TWO YOUNG WOMEN, a bit drunk, are on the sidewalk in front of me just now. There is a dude sitting on the bench at the bus stop, and he opens his mouth to speak as they pass by him.

Dark-haired woman puts her hand up in his face. "DO NOT EVEN START WITH WHATEVER STUPID SHIT YOU WERE JUST GOING TO SAY TO US," she yells at him.

He shuts his mouth. An old woman sitting on the other end of the bench gives both young women a thumbs-up. Dude says nothing. Old lady smiles. I crack up, audibly.

Dark-haired woman turns to me. "FUCK YOU LAUGHING ABOUT? YOU'RE NEXT, BUDDY."

TODAY, AT NINE in the morning, I saw a woman walking her chihuahua in a bedazzled housecoat and furry high heels. And her nightgown. Drinking her coffee and smoking a cigarette. I salute her.

TODAY I WAS walking up the street and, as they were passing me going the other way, I heard a kid about seven years old say to her mother, "I don't know why he was being such a dick."

Mom said, "You shouldn't call other kids that."

Kid said, "Okay, then, I don't know why he was being such an asshole."

That's all I heard. Been laughing about it all day.

LAST SATURDAY I was waiting outside my building for my bandmates to come pick me up to head out of town for a gig.

An old man slowly walked up the hill, and then stopped in front of me. "Is that a tenor saxophone you have there?" he asked, pointing at my horn case.

I nodded.

"You on your way to play a show?" he asked.

I said, "Yes. Yes I am."

His face lit up. "I played the tenor saxophone all my life, until this happened," he exclaimed, pulling his hand out of the pocket of his coat. It was pretty mangled, like maybe from an industrial accident of some kind. "I love the saxophone," he told me. Slipped his hand back into his pocket. "You go and play your heart out tonight, son. You play that horn for both of us, you hear me?"

I told him, "Yes, sir, I will." And so I did.

CORNER OF CLARK and Venables. I'm in my truck, waiting for the light. I notice a very beautiful femme I have seen out at a few events crossing the street. Two dudes in the lane beside me have their windows down and they catcall something at her that I can't make out. She pretends to clean her ear with her middle finger, like she can't quite hear them, and then gives them the same middle finger. So badass.

5. THERE

I HAD STRESS travel dreams all last night. I had four carry-on bags. I was travelling with fifteen people who were all late types. We nearly missed our overseas flight, but it was delayed. Then my bags were lost, and mine were the only ones missing. Maybe I won't compile all my calendar updates right before bed again. Maybe that's a morning activity.

ME: "I SURE get a lot of these pat-downs. These machines hate me because I'm trans. Did you press the pink or the blue button?"

Canadian Air Transport Security Authority guard: "These machines hate me too, because I'm covered in piercings and I have four screws in my leg. There's no button for that, either."

FLIGHT ATTENDANT: "CAN I get you anything to drink, sir? Oh, pardon me, ma'am. I'm so sorry."

Me: "It's totally okay. I prefer sir, actually."

Him: "Of course. Yes, ma'am."

Me: "I prefer sir, though."

Him: "Of course. I'm sorry again, ma'am."

Me: (Sigh) "I would love a black coffee with one sugar, please."

Him: "Yes, ma'am. Coming right up."

THE WOMAN ACROSS the aisle from me on the plane is having a giant coughing attack.

The man beside her is visibly disgusted. "You shouldn't get on a plane when you're sick like that. You'll spread those germs everywhere."

She looks at him deadpan. "I have lung cancer," she tells him. "It's not contagious. Though some days I wish it was. Selectively."

TODAY AT TORONTO Pearson airport, I get on the train between terminals with a young woman, her maybe five-year-old daughter, and three airplane pilots, one female and two male.

The little girl clocks the female pilot, looks her up and down. "Are you a lady pilot?" she asks, very excited.

The female pilot smiles and says yes, she is.

The little girl is bouncing on her toes now. "That is sooooo cool! Like, do you ever fly a jet plane?"

The pilot nods and smiles.

The girl's mother looks at the two male pilots and says to them, "It's cool that you both fly planes too. It's just as cool."

The little girl shakes her head emphatically and says, super loud: "No, it's not. It's waaaay better when SHE does it. Look! She has gold things on her shirt, just like a soldier. She can probably just fly anywhere."

I'M IN A shuttle van in Ontario at nearly two a.m. and the driver's got the eighties channel on the radio and it's playing "Jump" by Van Halen, and I swear, Kim-Marie Rumley, I'm having a hard-core flashback to that sleepover party at Denise Lloyd's on the hot springs road when all of us were still young and alive, and no one was divorced yet except some of our parents.

FLYING TO CALGARY, no checked luggage. I am waiting for my suitcase to go through the X-ray, when I see on the screen a giant dildo in someone's carry-on bag. I glance nonchalantly at the woman beside me, and then at the man on the other side of me. Neither appears to notice anything. Then I realize that is MY bag up on the screen. At first I am very confused, having just packed my bag for a solo overnight work gig in Alberta, as a speaker for an interfaith religious conference of all things, and I know for sure my bag is sans dildo of any kind. The dude is looking at me. The woman is trying not to crack even a tiny smile. The technician is now looking at me as well.

"It's a microphone," I say to nobody and everybody at the same time. "It's a vocal microphone."

Nobody says anything.

"Microphone!" I repeat.

LAST FALL I was flying home after doing a storytelling festival in Montreal. The festival had booked me on a cruelly early flight, so I was lined up to go through security at about 4:30 in the morning.

It was pretty quiet still, a Monday, so there were a lot of business dudes in suits, and me.

The security guard looked like she was about eighteen and had borrowed her uniform from her older brother. She explained that I had been selected for a random secondary search. She motioned to her male co-worker to come over and pat me down, so I cleared my throat and spoke up.

"So, I guess this is where I should tell you that I am trans," I said.

This was when she did something that it would be way easier to physically perform than it will be to capture in a word cage, but I will try to describe it anyway: First, she made a kind of one-person wave with her tiny body that started in her feet and undulated up to her shoulders. Then her legs and arms sort of ran away from her torso for a millisecond, and then returned, while her feet remained planted in her scuffed black uniform boots. She lifted both arms, and then dropped them again, her metal detector wand hanging limp against her thigh. Her eyebrows were raised like umbrellas above her over-wide eyes. She swallowed twice but did not blink.

"That's okay," she reassured me, though it was painfully apparent none of this was in any way okay with her.

"Thank you," I said. "I know it's okay." I was trying not to smile, quite sure she was not as ready to find any of this as funny as I did.

"Okay, then." She took a deep breath and looked up and to the right, like she was taking an exam and trying to remember the correct answer. "Here is what is going to happen. My colleague is going to inspect the parts of you that are male, and then I"—she lifted her wand, just a little—"will inspect the parts of you that are female." She looked over at her co-worker. He was standing with his head cocked, waiting, unsure.

A small crowd of businessmen were gathering behind me, sighing and looking at their phones.

I opened my passport and showed her the picture page, showed her the *F* there. I was really trying not to laugh out loud now. "I know my rights." My words were slow, and calm. I know what happens to people who get angry in airports. It never goes their way. "My reward for being trans in an airport is not an extra pat-down. The rules are that everyone has the right to be searched by someone of their same gender." I allowed a tiny smirk to pull at one corner of my mouth. "But it is four-thirty in the morning, so good luck finding someone of my gender here right now. So I get to choose who I feel more comfortable being patted down by, and if it's okay with you, if you consent, then I pick you."

She nodded repeatedly, like she had just been told by the swim teacher that it was her turn to jump off the really high diving board.

She wafted her wand over my waistband, and then pinched it between her knees to free up both of her hands. She took a deep breath and then patted my flat chest with the backs of both of her hands once, like she was touching something dangerously hot with no oven mitts, and then stepped back and motioned for me to proceed.

"Thank you," she said, without looking up, without meeting my eyes. Without ever smiling.

Yesterday I met a woman named Hue. She worked in the housekeeping department at the hotel I was staying at. I was on my way to teach a workshop, and when I came out of my room, she said, "Hi, Ivan, how is your day?"

So I asked her how did she know my name, and what was her name?

The hotel gives her a report with all the guests' names, she said, and she just remembers them. She has worked here for twenty-nine years, she told me.

She looked too young for that to be possible, so I said, "What, were you ten when you started here?"

She laughed and waved me away with her hand. "I'm forty-nine!" she told me.

"So am I!" I said.

"Nineteen sixty-nine?" we said at the same time and laughed, and she gave me a high-five.

"That's impressive that you remembered my name," I said. "I'll leave you a good tip when I check out."

She shook her head, said she doesn't work tomorrow, she has Thanksgiving off.

"Should I just give it to you now?" I said.

She nodded quickly, and so I did.

I'M AT THE very swank hotel where the Melbourne Writers Festival is hosting the authors. Tonight, the ballroom downstairs is hosting the Miss Australia beauty pageant gala. This is making for some strange mingling in the hotel lobby. There is a story here for sure; I just don't know what it is yet. I just walked through a cluster of sequined gowns and tuxedos in my gym clothes, for starters.

YESTERDAY I WAS hassled again in a women's bathroom, by a staff member of the restaurant I had just eaten in. She questioned me, and then left to gather a group of male staff to confront me. Here's the thing about when this stuff happens: in addition to making me feel unwelcome and uncomfortable (and sometimes even unsafe) in a so-called public place, often the person doing the hassling is not only assuming that I am a man in the women's bathroom but also inferring that I am there to do harm to women and/or children. So if I seem offended when this happens, it is probably because I am. It is this assumption of ill intent that really gets me. So much more hurtful than the plain old silly-man-can't-read-the-sign version.

ON THE FERRY this evening I'm waiting outside the gender-neutral/ accessible bathroom for nearly twenty minutes when a staff guy comes out of a nearby office.

"Is this the only gender-neutral bathroom on this boat?" I ask him.

"Yes," he tells me. "We are just transitioning." He looks uncomfortable for a second. "Uh, I mean, it's a transition period. We are, uh, undergoing a period ... of change. We're trying to, uh, change. Be better. With this stuff."

I smile.

He looks relieved.

So what, burly dude smoking on the ferry deck? So I screamed a little. So maybe it was more like a screech. So would you if a giant moth flew into your eye and then down the front of your shirt BEFORE you had even identified what it was. It was the not-knowing bit that threw me. Also, moths freak me out a little. So much more aggressive and random than their cousins: like a drunk butterfly, on a couple lines of coke.

I **AM IN** Port Alberni on Vancouver Island for a festival this weekend. A long way from a Pride parade. Still, I see a pretty boy swishing his way through the hotel parking lot just now when I go out for a walk.

"Good evening, fine sir," he says to me, as we pass each other.

"Why thank you, m'lady," I say to him.

Then we both smile, and he blows me a kiss, and then curtsies. I tip my imaginary hat. It is beautiful, and perfect.

A TEAM OF DRUNK twentysomething girls with wash-off dragon and unicorn tattoos are cruising me on this plane to Sudbury. The plane smells like cigarettes and has a PROPELLER, which is making a strange noise. Great. Now I'm homesick for the Yukon.

"**Nobody swims in** the lake," the waitress Tracie with an IE tells me. "Nobody. I've never swum in Williams Lake, and I've lived here all my life."

Tracie's dad owns the place, and she remembers me from last time.

"Because of the mill?" I ask her.

"They say it's more the sewage. From ages ago."

"Are things harder here after the fire?"

"Which one?" she asks me. "There's fires every summer now. But you know what? The people who lost their houses aren't the ones complaining about it. It's the people whose houses weren't touched by any fires who say this town is so much worse now. It's the people who never lost nothing saying those fires ruined this town." She shakes her head. "You want more coffee? I can put on some fresh."

DAWSON CREEK. I'M surrounded by femme tomboys. My gran used to call them tough broads. Eyeshadow and coveralls. Manicures and steel-toed boots. It's nice to be north.

TODAY AT MY gig at the Moose Jaw Pride lunch in the basement of the United Church I met a woman named Jean. She was in her mid-eighties, maybe even nineties, I would say. She had a walker. She waited to talk to me.

"I'm here because I used to have a granddaughter," she told me. "And now I have a grandson. I came to listen to you. They say you can't teach an old dog, but here I am, learning. He's an engineer. We're all very proud of him. He's done so well. God bless you, and God bless your stories, too. I went to the flag raising in the park last night and got invited to this, and so here I am."

I asked her if she was a hugger, and she told me she sure was. She said God bless me about four or five times. I will never forget Jean from Moose Jaw. She gives really good hugs, too.

You want to hear the other story that happened to me in Moose Jaw? I got called a dyke bitch in the elevator at the hotel. No one wants to hear that story, though. But that happened, too. I never once felt safe on the streets in that town, night or day, but that is so normal it's not even a story. But it's true.

THEY ARE VERY concerned about flooding this spring here in Winnipeg. I heard a guy on the radio today praying for what he called a gentle melt. I can't stop thinking about this term, how much I like it, and how I need to adopt this idea, like, metaphorically speaking, into how I go about living life in general.

WHEN YOU ARE riding on a San Francisco Muni bus and it starts up a hill, a calm woman's voice comes over the intercom and says "Please hold on" in a firm yet reassuring fashion. I am going to try to record it on my phone tomorrow so that I can listen to it all the time, no matter where I am. I think that would be good for me.

SOMETIMES THERE YOU are on the highway, and you drive right through a flock of memories, like ghosts. All you can do is keep your eyes on the road.

6. REBENT SINNER

FROM ABOUT 1997 to 2003 or so, I worked in the film industry, first as a lamp operator, and then as a props person.

We shot a lot in Vancouver's Downtown Eastside, a neighbourhood made infamous by the media, mostly because of the missing and murdered largely Indigenous sex workers who disappeared from its streets in the late 1980s, throughout the '90s, and into the early 2000s, whose remains were discovered in 2002 on a pig farm in Port Coquitlam. More recently, the Downtown Eastside is known for what can only be called rampant gentrification of a part of the city that once, for all its complicated faults, contained the bulk of this increasingly unlivable city's cheap and low-barrier housing.

When we used to shoot movies down there I was always troubled by the waste and flash of the movie business clashing with the poverty and need of our city's homeless and addicted. I remember getting a memo from the production office of a TV series I worked on reminding us not to share our lunch with any of the residents, in case it invited even more crime to set.

I mostly worked on the props truck, and I always arrived early, to drink coffee and get myself organized and prepared for the weird hustle-and-wait pace of a day on location. Nearly every morning, when I got to my five-ton props truck at or just before dawn, there would be little rectangular signs, cut out of plastic foam core, or sometimes soggy cardboard, placed carefully under the windshield wipers or tucked under the padlock and latch for the back sliding door. The signs were always hand lettered, always in the same careful, rounded cursive, and they always contained only two words, the first in red ink and the second in black: *Repent Sinner.* Hundreds of them over the years, left all over the city.

But no one ever witnessed the person who created and left them. There were rumours that it was an older homeless woman, and I even spotted her one morning, disappearing down an alley like a phantom, the little signs peppered behind her, but I never actually saw her leave one.

One morning I found one propped on the tailgate. It appeared after I had already been to the props truck and hauled the on-set cart down the alley and up the elevator in the then-unrenovated Woodward's Building, left it on set, and then returned to the truck. This sign was a little different from the others, though, like someone had bumped its creator's hand mid-letter, and the *p* in *repent* had a little dog ear sticking up out of the top of it. At first glance, it looked like it said *rebent*, not *repent.*

Rebent Sinner. I read it aloud to myself and laughed, took it home with me that night in my backpack and thumbtacked it to the corkboard above my desk.

Rebent Sinner. *That is my new motto,* I thought, every time I sat down at that desk to write, until that desk and that wall and that corkboard and that sign were destroyed in a house fire in 2005.

It's a great name for a book, I thought.

So I GO into one of those outdoor stores because I'm looking for a pink plaid shirt, and there is a dude in there trying on hats.

He says to another customer, "My wife is not here and I need a woman's opinion on this hat. What do you think?"

She shakes her head at him and indicates she doesn't speak English. She obviously has no idea what he is on about and appears a little uncomfortable. She walks away.

He looks at me.

"I think that hat looks good on you," I say.

"Yeah, but I need a female perspective," he says.

"Well, technically, I was assigned female at birth, and I think the hat looks good on you." I smile at him.

"Well, I need more of a ... woman's perspective."

I probably should have ended our conversation there, but for some reason, I doubled down on him. Some days I can't help myself; I'm not even sure why. "Well, I've got my period right now, and my perspective is you should wear whatever hat you like the best, no matter what any perfect stranger who happens to be a woman in here says about it," I say, still smiling.

"And that is why I'm not asking you," he says.

Now I notice there is an older woman standing there, too. I'm unsure how much of the conversation she has overheard.

"I think that hat makes your head look very, very small," she tells the guy, whirls on one heel of her Birkenstock, and then winks at me and walks away.

I'm still laughing about it, several hours later.

TODAY I CALLED a spa to find out whether they had any gender-neutral change rooms and was asked, "Are you American? Because in Canada everybody is pretty cool about that stuff." (Not relaxing for me. Just FYI, full-speed-ahead denial is not helpful.)

Sigh.

So right after that I went to trans-inclusive swim (which also welcomes family and allies) at Templeton pool for some safe swimming time.

First, I want to thank all the folks who fought and worked to make this space happen for us. It really, really is a healing place for me. I am a water baby, always have been, and pools and beaches can be hard for me to navigate. I love trans swim.

My thoughts:

Some trans people show up to spaces like these after a lifetime of anxiety, fear, and even dangerous moments in change rooms and sports facilities.

We need to welcome each other when we get here. We need to smile and be kind. If you can, and if they seem open, say hello and introduce yourself. Because othering or excluding other trans folks in spaces that are supposed to be safe(r) is potentially really hurtful. They might not ever come back, and that is a tragedy. A kind of silent violence maybe even. From our own kind, to each other. A space is only as safe and welcoming as we all make it.

I say this as someone who is often managing my own anxiety, my own shyness.

Also, next Sunday is bouncy castle day at Templeton pool. 11:30 to 1:30. If you come, I promise to say hi.

THE PEOPLE ASKING if a nine-year-old kid can even know that he is gay should be asking how the other nine-year-olds already know to bully him for coming out.

I DON'T CARE what Rotten Tomatoes says. *Cat People* (1982) with Nastassja Kinski totally stands the test of time, ever since it first freaked the living shit out of me while also strangely being hot that night I was babysitting in grade nine on Clyde Wann Road in Porter Creek, the end, a story by Ivan.

I USE THE pronoun they. I am used to people using both he and she to refer to me, and I have used both pronouns for myself for different reasons in the past, before I knew about the they pronoun. I make myself be okay with people using either pronoun for me most days, mostly because I don't want how my day goes to be decided by others' language too, too much.

But I use the pronoun they, and the added respect and feeling "seen" I experience when people get it right feels so good and accurate and true to me. I really appreciate those people who ask, who learn it and then do it, especially when they just do it and don't turn it into a production. Like, I really appreciate it.

Don't bite the effing rainbow-filled Oreo, people. It's a trick. Smoke and mirrors. Until a gay boy wearing eyeliner can walk safely up Commercial Drive in Vancouver right after Italy wins a soccer match, and our kids don't get harassed trying to get an education, and young lesbian couples are not shot in parks in Texas, and there is no death penalty anywhere for being queer, and everyone can piss in a public washroom without hassle or fear, then I will swallow no rainbow cookie. Plus, think of the chemicals in those things.

It's ALL WELL and good to say what you think. But the catch here is that this, by definition, requires that you think before actually saying anything.

A FRIEND TOLD me today, "Don't catch a falling cactus." I did this only once, but still, it needs remembering.

IF HE IS a lone wolf, then why are there so many of him?

LET'S JUST MAKE one thing perfectly clear. We're not asking for a special washroom. If a public building only has gendered washrooms, what that actually means is that women and girls have a special bathroom and men and boys have a special bathroom. Most of the time, everybody but trans people have special bathrooms.

It's not a special bathroom. You can use it, too. And you. You're all welcome in there. We would never keep anyone out of the bathroom because of their gender, or what kind of clothes they are wearing. I mean, seriously, what kind of an asshole would do something like that?

I want you to know that trans people, we don't get up in the morning and make menacing steeple shapes with our unusually long and graceful fingers and plot new and creative ways to throw a sparkle-encrusted wrench into the engine room of your perfectly tuned gender binary. We really don't. We are just trying to go to school, or go swimming, or use the weight room without being hassled. Just like you.

ON APRIL 19, 2016, I was walking from my apartment to the market along a very busy street in East Vancouver. About a half block up the street I saw something that just seemed a little off to me somehow. Maybe it was a body-language thing, maybe it was my trans person's heightened spidey sense when it comes to anticipating potential violence or danger, but I noticed an interaction that seemed wrong. And I wasn't wrong.

A very large man was looming over a woman sitting on a bus stop bench. She was young, maybe nineteen or twenty, and wearing a sleeveless floral dress. She had headphones in her ears and appeared to be trying to read a book.

The man weighed about 130 kilos (280 pounds) and was in his late forties, easy. He was so angry his face was a tomato, and he was screaming right into her face, spraying spit everywhere. As I got closer, I could hear what he was saying.

"What the fuck is wrong with you? Why can't you even say hello to me? Bitch. You're a stuck-up little bitch."

The young woman was shaking and silent.

I was about to intervene, but I was intercepted by a tiny and fierce woman in her early eighties, I would say, who squared off and gave the man a solid tongue-lashing in a heavy accent, wagging her finger and saying he was twice her age and twice her size, and did his mother know he roamed the streets talking to ladies like this?

He sneered and called her a dried-up old cunt.

That's when I swallowed and stepped up, saying no, no, he couldn't speak to anyone like that.

"Stay out of this, faggot," he said, and pulled his ham-shaped fist back. But then the bus pulled up, and he turned and got on it.

The young woman did not. She watched the bus pull into traffic, and then turned to the old woman and me, and burst into tears.

"Oh my God, thank you both so much. I knew it. I should have just worn a flour sack or something, but I had a job interview. I just wanted to look nice, you know? I want this job so bad. I need to get out of my parents' place and move into the city. That was the third time it's happened to me today, and you were the only ones who said anything. One dude followed me right off the train, all the way down the block. I was so afraid and nobody helped me until now. Next time, I will wear a flour sack to take the bus and get changed when I get there."

We all exchanged names and hugs. We told Alicia from the suburbs that she should be able to wear whatever she wanted and take the bus unmolested. Maria from Costa Rica told me I was a nice gentleman and I did not correct her.

When I got home, I wrote a quick little post for my public author page, something to the effect of: Dear dudes (yes, all men): She's wearing headphones AND reading a book. This is code for she is not interested. She is not obligated to smile at you. If she's being polite to you, it might be because she knows that if she isn't, you might get nasty, even violent, and this is a lesson she was taught as a very little girl. She's not wearing that dress for you. She's not on the bus to meet men; it's public transit. Leave her alone. Tell your friends.

I hit post and forgot about it.

Until about an hour later, when I picked up my phone and it said I had

2,000 notifications. Within a couple of hours my post had gone viral, and over the next few days it was reposted or written about on Boing Boing and Reddit and HuffPost, and translated into Spanish and Portuguese and French and Czech and Russian. Media contacted me for quotes.

I was invited by a Russian feminist discussion group to Skype in to one of their meetings. They really wanted to speak to a feminist man, they wrote me. I said sure, but I didn't identify as a man. I was a non-binary trans person, I told them. "Oh," they replied. "Then we are not interested."

That short, unedited, nearly punctuationless post of mine has now been viewed more than any other string of words I have ever written in any of my eleven books over two decades of writing and publishing has ever been read, ever. In retrospect, I wish I had considered paragraph or line breaks, but who knew?

In the midst of it all came the abuse. The men's rights activist army was deployed. Thousands and thousands of comments and emails and tweets from men who took issue with anyone saying that they did not have the right to the time and attention of any woman in public, anytime, anywhere. Most of them assumed I was a man, and a man saying these things to other men sent them into a kind of collective fury and rage. Vitriol. Threats of violence. Dick pics. Disgusting screen caps of women's faces with ejaculate all over them. I got death threats. Slurs. Levelled not just at me but also at the many, many women and girls commenting on my page. Jokes about the size of my penis. I had to look up the words "chode" and "cuck" and "neckbeard" and "white knight." My favourite insult was dickless wonder. I think that would make a great T-shirt slogan, right? I like it. Dickless Wonder, that's me.

But from the midst of the misogyny and entitlement and abuse there emerged a vital conversation. Women telling their own stories about unsolicited attention. On buses and streets, at work, in parks, on airplanes and trains and everywhere. It started when they were ten or eleven, some women said. It happens every day, they said. A real and powerful and painful conversation grew by the minute. I was moved and awed and honoured to host it.

I became a kind of accidental moderator. I wanted the conversation to be kept safe enough for women to come and share their stories. I deleted any comment that included the word "pussy" or "bitch" or "cunt" or "faggot" or "feminazi." I erased anything that included a rape threat or was overtly rude. Hundreds and hundreds a day. I got a repetitive strain injury that still ails me to this day (they call it Millennial Thumb) from swiping and hitting ban and delete so many times on my iPhone. Every morning upon waking, I would delete nasty comments for a couple of hours, and then several times during the day. The misogynists were especially active in Europe and Australia during the Canadian night.

One morning I awoke to an email that read "I Love Dick" in the subject line. I sighed and swiped left to delete it, but luckily, something else caught my eye. "New Amazon television series by creator of *Transparent*, Jill Soloway."

Apparently, she had seen me on YouTube or somewhere and she wanted me to audition to play the part of, get this, a butch writer living in an Airstream trailer. *Play?* I thought. I was perfect for this role. I would be playing Kevin Bacon's love rival. *Story of my life!* I thought.

I enlisted the help of an actor friend to coach me for my big audition.

But I never heard back, so I can only assume at this point that I did not get the part.

And that is totally okay, because just a couple of days ago, my original post was picked up again by a huge online feminist news site, and the slew of abusive comments and name-calling has begun anew.

So I know my shot at the Hollywood big time will be coming around again soon. Anytime now I will get the audition call.

Orange Is the New Black and *The Handmaid's Tale*, I await your correspondence.

And this time, I am ready. I am changed.

This is what I learned: I look like a man to most people in my tiny profile picture on social media. Men get listened to by default, even when they are talking over women who are speaking about their own lived experiences. If I presented as more feminine, my post never would have gone viral. I was perceived by most to be a man speaking to other men. Most men don't respond well to this. The consequences are scorn and dismissal and threats and even violence for men who speak up and challenge their sense of entitlement to the time and space and attention of women and girls. The system polices itself and punishes any man who questions it. Men who don't play along are seen as not real men. I used to wonder why so many men stay silent when witnessing harassment, but I don't anymore. I do not accept this as an excuse, but I do acknowledge it as an explanation. My own masculine presentation has allowed me to see the insides of the machine. Most of the men who came after me called me queer or accused me of speaking up only to garner favour with women. The possibility that a real man would step up and speak against harassing women on the street simply because it is wrong was not even a plausible option for them. I had to have another, more sinister motive.

The whole experience rattled the ghost of the little girl I once was, and shook loose my own stories, and my own scars. It also made me flip over my own masculine privilege and examine it, take it apart, and study the pieces. I'm putting it back together slowly and, I hope, leaving some of those pieces out. Butches and trans masculine people, especially of my age, have not been afforded many healthy role models when it comes to constructing our own masculinities, and we often assemble ourselves around the remains of our own traumas and still-screaming memories of failed attempts at being feminine. So we stumble and falter and overcompensate and build our identities without any blueprints. The result can be a flawed foundation, and the cracks in it sometimes leak, and bleed with our own complicity.

Being masculine in a female-assigned body is not an escape hatch that lets me avoid male violence and harassment. It is a window, and it allows me to look out, but it also obligates me to look in.

THIS POST IS performing better than eighty percent of everything else you have ever written in your life. Boost it to show more people that you're not just a hack wasting everybody's time.

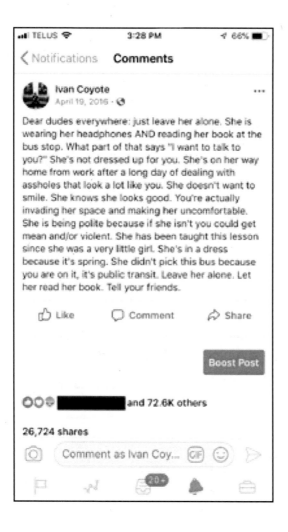

FLAGGING HAS NEVER gone out. Should never, ever be allowed to go out. May all the secret languages of the queers and the bent live on in our pockets forever.

7. SHOW AND TELL

I'M CHANGING MY pronoun to sheimeanhesorrythey just to make things easier for hosts at literary events to introduce me.

A FEW YEARS ago I had the great fortune to be invited to a writers festival. I said yes as soon as I heard that my friend and fellow writer Richard Wagamese was also going to be there. I had met him years ago at another festival and we had recognized each other immediately, as heart-born storytellers always do.

Richard and I walked each day to and from the motel and the venue along the beach and talked. He was the only First Nations writer at the festival, and I was the only trans person there, as a writer, or even as an audience member, as far as I could tell or feel, though you can't always tell, you can't always feel. There was no gender-neutral bathroom at the venue, and on the first night, a woman in the bathroom screeched at me, just minutes before I had to step onstage. I sold that same woman a book after the show, and neither of us mentioned the incident in the bathroom.

Anyhow. Richard and I had been programmed together for an event on the closing night, to interview each other and do short readings.

"Don't you think that's weird, Richard?" I asked him. "It is no coincidence that they put the only First Nations guy and the only trans person together, right? It's like one of those diversity panels."

"No coincidence at all, Coyote," he said to me. "But who else will tell our stories for us but us? I would rather be interviewed by someone who has at least some mirrored experience of being the other, of always being the only one in the room. I'm glad it will be you asking me questions tonight, fellow misfit, fellow ambassador, fellow teacher. Our job is to see this as an honour, not a chore. That will make us so much better at it."

TONIGHT AFTER MY show, one of the first people in line to get her book signed leaned in and told me she didn't want to use the they pronoun for me, because she didn't, and I quote, "want to lose me." And then she basically harangued me about going into schools, because if I was not using the she pronoun anymore, then what kind of a role model was I for all those girls now? All of this with a long line behind her of other folks waiting to speak to me or have their books signed. I didn't even know what to say to her. Other than, of course, the ninety-minute show where I had just poured my heart out about my time in the gender trenches.

The silver lining?

The sixty-something-year-old, very straight, conservative-looking dude who sat in the front row and nodded, smiled, and even rocked out through the whole show. He shook my hand afterward and said, "Good stuff. My wife and I, we just love your work. We hope you never stop."

OKAY, TO BE honest, I was not thinking this gig in Coquitlam was going to be a fun one for me. The stage was running half an hour late, so there was lots of bleed from the mainstage rock band to fight sound over, an unfocused crowd in and out of the tent, and a giant group of old women who were just in the tent because it was cooler inside in the shade and there were chairs and no infernal rock music.

So. One of those old women (late eighties, I would guess but did not ask) bought a book after. I signed it to Margaret.

What she really wanted was a *Tomboy Survival Guide* postcard, she told me. "I need one or two of these. I was a tomboy way back in the day. Thank you. I was not as lucky as you. I had it pounded and prayed out of me, just like you said in your story."

She looked me in the eye and started to cry. So did I. I asked Margaret if I could give her a hug.

"Oh, by all means," said Bernice, sitting right behind her in a motorized chair. "She loves hugging. We're together."

Then Margaret and I gave each other a long, deep soul hug. She was still crying.

"I don't think they pounded and prayed it right out of you," I told her.

She shook her head and nodded, kind of at the same time. She was wearing a baby-blue blouse and a butterfly brooch.

So, here is to all the Margarets and Bernices out there. I am grateful that my art sometimes helps us find each other, sometimes in the last places either of us were looking.

ABOUT FORTY KIDS did a circus show to open for my reading tonight. I didn't take a single picture because I just wanted to be there and witness it. It was beautiful and powerful and mighty. I can now say that I have performed after an act that closed with a team of synchronized Hula Hoopers and kids in tiger suits jumping through said hoops to AC/DC's "Back in Black." I can finally say that. No tigers were harmed, the kids assured me. But the tigers did have to leave early because it was past their bedtime.

TONIGHT AFTER MY show, a woman in her seventies gave me a very solid hug, and then patted my cheek and told me I was a tender gentleman.

I'M IN THE parking lot of a park in Coquitlam where they are having an arts festival where I'm about to do my last gig before a month off from performing.

Artist's liaison says to me on the phone: "I will come and meet you there and take you to the Story Café."

Me: "I will be the butchy one by the silver truck. I'm wearing a blue shirt. And, uh, blue pants and blue shoes. And, well, blue socks and underwear, too."

Artist liaison: "I should be able to locate you before we get to the underwear bit."

Dear Journalist:

It's not that I don't trust you, personally. I am sure you are a kind, compassionate human who got into the field for all the right reasons. I am sure you have at least skimmed the book of mine you were assigned to review. I am sure you will make a decent attempt to understand me and what I am trying to say.

It's just that I have been burned so very many times before. By journalists who didn't read the book, who don't care, who have misquoted or misunderstood me. By editors who changed pronouns, who got it wrong, who called me nonsensical and non-consensual names like gender blender.

That is why I insist on writing my answers to you in an email. That is why I don't trust you to "jot down some notes" and get it right. We are talking about gender here. It is complicated. It is important. There are so many ways to not get this right, including the ones you are about to invent and excuse yourself for after the fact, when it is too late and cannot be unprinted.

So don't take it personally if I handle you and your pen like a venomous snake. It's not about you.

Love, Ivan.

SOMETIMES YOU JUST have to stand up there and tell your queer story in front of mostly cis and straight people. You just gotta do it, or else nothing's ever going to change as big as we need it to. And sometimes they will laugh in the right places, but you won't truly know if they are loving you or eating your difference. You just gotta do it, but that doesn't mean I don't get to say how tired I feel after.

B. CLASS

TODAY WAS THE most physically demanding day of this chunk of school gigs. Three shows in three different towns, plus solo driving.

First thing this morning a teacher whispered to me, just before I performed for 400 kids, that one of his grade tens' dads had just called the school and pulled his son out of my show because "it might promote a message I don't agree with."

My show is tame. The message is pretty much to get the kids to think about the consequences of cruelty and bullying. Sometimes parents google me, though, and make assumptions about my school material, I think because I am trans.

The principal was a good guy, it seemed, and he walked me out to my truck after the show. He said he wanted to follow up with that parent and tell him what a valuable opportunity his kid had missed, and how if his son had been allowed to attend and ask questions, it might have spurred valuable conversation about important issues.

I told the principal I sure hoped the kid wasn't queer or trans, because then they might really be struggling, with no support at home.

His eyes filled with tears. "God," he said. "I didn't even think about that. I couldn't even let myself go there."

I said, "Next time I come, if anything like that happens again, invite the parent and the kid to come together, and tell them they are free to leave at any time without judgment from me if the parent disagrees with my message."

"Let's do that," he said, and hugged me really hard. He made me a really good coffee, too, for the road.

TODAY AFTER MY school gig, I had a special meeting arranged by the vice-principal with a trans kid in grade eight. A healthy, happy, articulate, smart, and handsome trans kid. He said his mom was supportive, and his stepdad treated him like his own son. He said the school was doing a good job of supporting him. He said grade seven was the worst year of his life, but things were better now. We took some pictures together: he is cute as hell, and smiling.

TODAY AT MY school show, I met a tall and handsome, very gentle and sweet young man who told me he had just come out to his mom a couple of days ago and it went okay, but he did not feel he could come out to his father, maybe ever. He said he was the oldest male in his generation of his conservative Indian family, and there was a lot of pressure on him to get married and have kids.

"That could still happen," he told his mother. "It might just look different than you thought it would."

He said he had been in his school's gay-straight alliance club for several years and it had made his school life much better. "I just told my mom it was an anti-bullying club." He laughed.

"Yeah," I said. "I'm just here for my anti-bullying show."

We both cracked up.

After the show, he gave me three hugs. Three.

"Keep in touch," I told him, and I meant it. I hope he does. He was a beautiful gem, and I could see the heart in him sparkle from a mile away. I can still feel his heart, out there in the margins of Toronto somewhere, beating right alongside mine.

HIGH-SCHOOL GIG, FIRST thing in in the morning. Kid comes up to me at the break. Tells me the other kids get a cheap laugh from kicking her crutches out from under her. Tells me this is her first year in public school, that she was home-schooled before this. Because her parents didn't like the teachers. Because her parents didn't want the teachers and social services asking all those stupid questions.

"Like what questions?" I ask her.

"Oh, you know," she tells me. "All the usual questions."

I AM TEACHING a writing workshop to thirty grade twelve kids. We are doing a character-building exercise. They have created a character together: a twenty-nine-year-old virgin. I ask the kids to imagine what his secrets are and call them out, and I will write them on the board.

One kid yells out that our character is secretly a porn star.

"Okay," I say. "Except I thought we had already decided he was a virgin?"

The kid smiles a little, then answers me back totally deadpan: "Yeah," she says. "He's a soloist."

I nearly fell down laughing. Smart kids.

TODAY THE KID that broke my heart was sixteen. He waited to talk to me after the show and immediately started telling me about his physically abusive father, how he would hit him and spit in his face. There were other kids standing behind him, and they could hear him. I asked him to please pause so I could speak to the other kids first and make time after to speak to him alone.

After the other students left, he told me he was grateful for the privacy. "I don't talk about my life to anyone here," he said.

We sat and talked for about thirty minutes. He didn't want advice, he said. He didn't need to cry to a stranger, he said. I asked him if he thought tears were a sign of weakness. He admitted that he did.

"Who taught you that?" I asked him.

"My father," he said.

"Your father who you have already told me is not a good man? He forced you to control your tears as a little boy, yet he cannot control his own violence as a man? Is violence not a sign of weakness then, too? An inability to control oneself?"

I asked him if he had heard the term "toxic masculinity." He said no, but he could guess what it was and would look it up. He told me he felt angry nearly all the time but had learned to control it. He told me that he was okay with what his father did to him, that it made him strong. I told him I had a feeling that he was strong already.

"Do we really have to suffer to be strong?" I asked him.

He looked at his watch and apologized because he was late for class and had to go. "I hope you're not into hugging me now," he said, smiling a little.

I told him I felt like hugging him, but I could control it.

"Me too," he said, and put his backpack on and left.

I don't know what he wanted, and I don't know if I delivered. I don't know if I said any of the right things. Maybe it wasn't about what I said. Maybe it was more important for him to just tell someone. Just to talk and have somebody listen.

SOME DAYS I struggle with doing school shows. They're tiring and early and really, really hard work. I did three today. First 600 kids, then 700 kids, then 350 or so this afternoon.

I met this kid. She hand-drew and coloured this poster of Gendy the Unicorn for me to sign for her so it could be put up in the hall of her school.

And I met a different girl who was too terrified to come out to her evangelical father. She said she worried she would be homeless if she told him.

I told her what my grandmother once told me: "God doesn't make mistakes. You are exactly who you are meant to be. There is nothing sinful or unnatural about you. Nothing. Always remember that."

I also told her she didn't need to tell anyone if it would make her unsafe. She asked me for a hug and I gave her one. A long and really big hug. I should have thanked her for reminding me why I was there.

My sound guy for this morning's performance is named Nathan. He is twelve years old.

"I've got the settings just perfect," he tells me. "Just stay in the middle of the stage and you'll be good."

9. THE LAST TIME I SAW RICHARD

ONE: THE LAST TIME I SAW RICHARD

AN OLD FRIEND of mine recently broke up with her partner of twenty-seven years. They had to sell their house on the Island and split up all their finances, and go through nearly three decades of stuff they had collected together and divide all of that up too.

It was pretty rough, my friend told me, and weird, too, just how and what a person gets attached to over the years, without even realizing it, until you all of a sudden have to pack it, or throw it out, or give it away to someone you've somehow fallen out of love with. She said there was stuff she would rather throw out than leave to her ex, and that realization made her feel small, and unlovable. Like no one would ever love her again if they found out that truth about her, she told me.

"Anyways," she said, "enough about all that. Enough about my trivial nightmares. I've still got my health. Isn't that what everybody says in times like these? I've still got my health, and I've still got seven boxes of old papers from back in the day.," she told me over the phone. She's not one for texting, she always tells me when she calls. She just never took to it.

"Any fucking way," she said. "So, I'm going through all of this goddamn stuff. There's an entire tub of old photos, and you're in a bunch of them. Going way back, pal. Like, the Pride parade in 1989, it looks like? You were still a baby. The summer after the winter we first met. Skinny like a sapling. Fresh, right out of your wrapper. You were what, twenty years old, maybe? You want 'em? I know you don't have too many old photos left after your house fire. I need to unload most of it. No room for memories in a one-bedroom. I'm going to miss that fucking garage more than I ever will my ex-wife, I tell you that much."

She dropped those photos off last Labour Day long weekend. It was the third photo from the top that stopped me, heart like a hot rock in my chest and my mouth all dry and my eyes all wet.

Pride parade 1989. Vancouver. The photo had been taken by someone standing on the curb, probably my friend's ex-wife; she was always the one who had the camera slung around her neck back then.

I am marching with the ACT UP contingent. The AIDS Coalition to Unleash Power. AIDS activists walk, fists in the air behind a spray-painted *Silence = Death* banner with a bleeding pink triangle.

1989. I had come out of the closet only ten months prior to that day. It was my first ever Pride parade. Some of us felt like we were marching for our lives, and most of us really were. It was the pinnacle of the AIDS crisis: infection rates were on the rise, and Saint Paul's, in the heart of what we didn't call the Village yet, was the one hospital in the province with an AIDS ward. The government wouldn't pay for AZT, the only antiretroviral drug in town back then. People with HIV were being turned away from housing, schools, organized sports, being fired from restaurant jobs. The right-wing conservative evangelical Christian premier of the province had just proposed Bill C-34, which called to quarantine anyone with HIV. Fear and poverty were on everyone's tongues.

I was marching with about forty people, mostly gay men, almost all sporting at least one piece of black leather something. Leather chaps that were too big now. A leather vest dangling from a man's surfacing collarbones. What was his name? Kevin. He used to be a lawyer. He's gone now.

I ran my fingertip over all those faces. Matthew. He was Mohawk. Richard. Richard is still around. John.

I hadn't even thought about John in years. I searched his name on Facebook and found an archival video interview with him shot in 2014. So, he was still around four years ago. That didn't seem possible the last time I saw him, around 2011 or so, at another funeral, in his motorized chair. I almost hadn't recognized him, and he knew it, I could tell that he could tell.

"It's me, John," he said, and squeezed my hand with his impossibly long and slender fingers. "You probably don't recognize me with my beard all gone grey," he whispered, and winked.

I remember his hands were cold that day, and he let me warm them between mine in the faded lobby of the community centre.

I googled around to find something more recent about John. John couldn't be gone. He was too much of a shit disturber. I would have sensed a shift in the force if John were gone. Someone would have told me. He was always so fearless, chaining himself to the doors of politicians' offices and throwing red paint on Premier Bill Vander Zalm that infamous night outside the Queen Elizabeth Theatre. Blood on the hands of those who would not fund the few drugs that might help prolong the lives of the people who were sick. We chanted. We raged. We both got arrested that night, and released without our shoes into the alley behind the cop shop when it used to be at Main and Hastings.

John always said his secret to living with HIV and AIDS was to eat Kraft Dinner at least once a day, swore by it, and he had been diagnosed in 1984, before they even had a test for the antibodies. He had survived and thrived with full-blown AIDS for well over three decades, so nobody could argue with him about his Kraft Dinner theory. I stopped looking for John so I wouldn't have to find out that he was no longer to be found.

I searched through all the faces in that photograph. Some angry, some joyful, all determined.

All gone now, except me, and maybe John, and Richard.

I reminded myself to call Richard, invite him over to dinner or something. We will talk about his recent vacation to Palm Springs and where he had found a vintage pink tuxedo shirt and his shitty landlord and how he's thinking about moving to the Island still. And I will tell him I'm thinking about leaving the city, too. Come next June, I'm going home to the Yukon for the whole summer, and I feel good about it.

Yeah, I thought, I will have Richard over for dinner before I leave Vancouver, and I will not show him this photo of us from thirty years ago so we won't have to talk about how maybe it's just him and me still alive now to remember it all. We won't talk about how somehow it is thirty years later and maybe we are the only two faces left.

POSTSCRIPT

I CALLED UP a few folks and asked around some more about John.
He was spotted just last week smoking and telling jokes outside of
the Pumpjack Pub.

TWO: THIRTY-ONE YEARS NOW

IT'S COMING OUT Day today. I nearly forgot. It is October 12. On October 13, 1988, I kissed a girl for the first time.

I didn't even know I was queer until she kissed me. I was nineteen; she was twenty-eight. She was a jazz singer, and I played the saxophone. That was thirty-one years ago tomorrow. I can't believe it. We were the only two queers I knew.

We told her roommate, the actor, first. Her roommate's mom was a lesbian, so we went on a pilgrimage to meet the lesbians on their lesbian homestead on Vancouver Island. Where else? I am still friends with one of those women. The other has passed now, years ago, from a heart attack. I loved them both on sight. Still do. The First Lesbians I Ever Really Knew gave me two cassettes to play in my van: *Shadows on a Dime* by Ferron and *Joan Armatrading*, her self-titled album, the one with that song "Down to Zero" on it. I know every song on that record by heart, to this day.

So. Love to the jazz singer who kissed me, and love to her roommate, the actor with the lesbian mom, and love to the lesbian mom's lover, and finally, love to the lesbian mom, may she rest in power and live on in all of her children, one of whom I consider myself to be, in some small way.

I carry with me today a little part of each of them: in the corners of pockets in old coats, tucked into that drawer in the kitchen where you keep spare batteries and manuals, inside the stronger, stiffer silver hairs that grow now from my temples.

THREE: DEPARTURE GATE

AFTER TWENTY-FIVE YEARS of life mostly on the road, you get familiar with airports.

There's a waitress in the breakfast place in Ottawa who has outlasted three different name changes on the restaurant where she works the early-morning shift. Her name is Naz, and she knows I'm going to have black coffee and scrambled eggs and no toast. And I know she has three daughters and gets up at 3:45 a.m. every weekday to come to this job so she can be home at three p.m., when her kids get off school. Her middle daughter is a gymnast and her youngest loves to read and her oldest is obsessed with a white boy two years older than her who Naz has nicknamed Not Good Enough.

I know never to connect in Chicago in the winter months and to avoid the shrimp at the Thai place in the international terminal in Toronto.

I never forget my phone charger or my Kobo e-reader or my reusable water bottle because my shoulders know the feel of what my backpack weighs with everything in it.

Airports are the only place I ever see my friend the cello player and my other friend the famous young adult apocalyptic fiction author.

Anyhow. A couple of weeks ago, I was at the gate right next to the Starbucks in the domestic terminal of Vancouver International Airport when I spotted another queer in the crowd, tapping on her iPhone with a chewed-up forefinger. I had met her several times in Toronto, and we have many friends in common. I flipped through the Rolodex of names and faces in my head. Ella? No. Ava, her name was Ava.

She nodded hello and dragged her backpack off the seat next to her and deposited it between her Blundstones to make room for me to sit.

So I did.

We got to talking. She was coming back from Salt Spring Island, she told me, from seeing her terminally ill friend, probably for the last time. She was kind of like a surrogate matriarch for her, a chosen mother, and Ava was going to miss her, she said, but it had been so good to get to say a proper and intentional goodbye.

"She is kind of an elder to me," she said, and looked down at her boots, quiet for a beat. "I modelled myself after many bits of what she taught me, even though she was straight and vanilla and not an artist."

"Who are your queer elders?" I kind of blurted out, this half-formed question that had been rattling around in my own head and chest so much lately.

"My queer elders?" Ava said slowly, her forehead showing its lines. "I don't think I have any. Not really. I'm forty-six. Aren't I too old now to have queer elders?"

My eyes met hers. Her eyes were full of tears, and it was contagious.

She told me that she never really felt like she had a queer elder she could fully relate to, because she wasn't a butch, but she never felt she connected much to the word "femme," either.

I told her most of my queer male elders were dead, and that many of my lesbian elders turned out to be TERFs, so I had to turf them. We talked about me turning fifty, and her just turned forty-six, and how somehow, all of a sudden, there we were, looking around, and we were the oldest ones on the bill, the oldest one with paintings on the wall in the gallery, the oldest ones. How we would probably be the oldest ones at the dyke bar now, if there was still such a thing as a dyke bar, and if we ever actually went out to a bar anymore. We wondered how we could possibly turn into elders without help from actual elders. What would that even look like? How could we provide any wisdom at all without guidance?

Then they called us to board. We were in different boarding zones, and she was swallowed up by strangers. I didn't see her again when we landed in Toronto.

I revisited our conversation over and over in my head for days afterward, though, like my lips and teeth returning to a hangnail. I chewed it until it began to bleed a little.

I ran through the butches and femmes and trans men and non-binary people I had ever known who were older than me or wiser than me, or had come out before me or transitioned longer ago than I did.

Mary had three heart attacks and moved to the Sunshine Coast. The woman she sold her pet store to screwed her out of a bunch of money, and now she works part time in a shop in the ferry terminal to make ends meet.

Bet used to work at the longest-running lesbian centre in North America, until she was ousted from her position in the late-nineties and lambasted in the queer media by the much younger women who took over and then closed its admittedly imperfect doors forever less than a year later. Turns out those old dykes knew a thing or two about getting shit done that we forgot to learn from them before we discarded them for newer models.

Bet also moved to the Sunshine Coast and does home renovations to pay the bills. It took her ten years to recover from East Vancouver's queer community politics and begin to do any political activism again. She now works mostly with water protectors fighting the pipelines and rural voter registration. She is seventy-five years old and just had her heart broken again by an Australian woman whose affections faded somewhere between the first five-day fuck fest and the second nineteen-hour plane ride back to Canada, Bet told me when I called her out of the blue to catch up.

I was secretly thrilled when she told me that she just turned seventy-five and is still having five-day summer fuck fests with international strangers, but I didn't say so because I didn't want to seem insensitive given the latest developments in that relationship.

"It was one very long and awkward seven-day kayak trip, let me tell you," Bet said, and we both laughed.

I was also impressed that she is seventy-five and still going on seven-day kayak trips. I am turning fifty and wouldn't plan a seven-hour kayak trip, but I didn't say so because I didn't want to seem ageist, or lazy.

I hung up and looked at my list again. Catherine. Plane crash. I used to be able to talk to her about anything. And I do mean anything. She worked at Three Bridges health clinic and I once went to her for medical advice about a tragic anal tear situation that I was asking about for a friend.

"Tell your friend to take a laxative and take it easy for a couple of days." She laughed at me with those eyes. "Tell your friend not to put more on their plate than they can eat in one sitting."

Then I thought about Bear. The other Bear. Heart attack. Then there was Star. Suicide. Frances. Alzheimer's. Janine. I need to call and check in on Janine. Parkinson's.

Most of my American queer elders are dead now because of poverty and, until recently, no queer marriage, so no benefits and no health care, and that catches up to a person.

Except Jack. He is still around. Jack is a few months younger than my mom, so he is turning sixty-nine this December. He's had two minor strokes and lives in a subsidized seniors' housing unit in the suburbs of Seattle with his two fat cats. He custom-makes corsets and costumes for theatre and movies. He created all the dresses for all of the female characters on that TV series *Deadwood*. He was really proud of the fact that all the prostitutes' fancy dresses were made true to their time period. No zippers back then, he told me, so no zippers now. Eyelets and lace and hooks, instead. No plastic invented yet, so that is real whale bone in those corsets, he bragged. He calls me boyo and I call him Da, in honour of both our Irish blood. We usually talk a few times a year, on Father's Day, and Mother's Day, on his birthday and on the anniversary of the death of his only son, who was the only person on the planet who ever, ever called him Mom.

I forgot Kate. The writer. Two battles with cancer now, or has it been three? She once bought me a suit that fit me perfectly without any tailoring at all from a thrift store in Eugene for twenty-five bucks.

We were roommates at a writers' retreat in a cedar-and-glass lodge on the Oregon coast, and when I came out of the bathroom wearing my new-to-me suit, she screamed and clapped her hands and told me I looked like Brad Pitt. She said it was the best twenty-five bucks she had ever spent. We both marvelled at our good fortune to find a suit of such quality that fit twenty-four-year-old me. We wondered who it had originally belonged to. I found an envelope in the inside left jacket pocket with a faded card that said, *Congratulations, Jacob, on your bar mitzvah. Love, Aunt Felice and Uncle Stanley.* When I read the card to her, Kate laughed until her mascara ran and said my suit was even more perfect now.

Kate was the first trans person I ever saw naked who wasn't me. This turned out to be a much more important milestone than I was capable of realizing at the time.

Jim Deva used to be my dirty rotten cocksucking scoundrel role model until he fell off a ladder trimming a hedge on his lunch hour and broke his neck and died. It's been four years now and I'm still mad at him for that, even though one day I hope to die quickly doing something stupid that everyone told me I was too old to be doing for myself anymore.

I guess my only other elder was Leslie Feinberg, only we never met. S/he never friended me on Facebook and I never read hir Tweets or saw hir Instagrammed breakfast photographs.

But I read and then reread *Stone Butch Blues* in 1993, and found bits of myself in those words. Even though they were written by a big-city American butch about a world I would not even be born into for twenty more years, I recognized myself in someone else's story for the very first time.

I recognized myself and picked up a pen, and now it's twenty-seven years later and I have not put it down.

FOUR: HOW DARE YOU?

When I first started really writing, like for real writing, like not a story for English class or in a journal but for really real writing, *Stone Butch Blues* by Leslie Feinberg was the only book I could hold up and say, "I want to do this. I love this book because this is a story about someone like me, and before there was this book, there were no stories about people like me written by people like me. I want to write a book just like this one, except less sad. I want to be like the person in this book, except funnier. I want to write a book about this hard life, except I need this hard life to one day be easier."

Last year I got a letter (well, a Facebook message, actually) from a young trans guy who said he had read all my books, ever since he was in grade eight and a counsellor had given him one, and that my writing had given him hope, had helped him come out and transition and feel less alone, but now he was contacting me for the very first time ever to complain about something I had recently read at a live show I had done with some other writers. Their stuff was really heavy, he said, about sexual abuse and misogyny, and then I got up and told a funny story about how when I had top surgery, I was worried did they switch my nipples around and stitch the wrong one back on the right side or whatever, and how dare I make light of body dysmorphia issues like that and he was so disappointed and so forth, and P.S.: Why didn't I also talk about capitalism and the environment and other important issues?

I called another writer friend of mine and read her the message.

I was nearly in tears, and she was trying not to laugh at me but not succeeding. She has three books out and is working on her fourth, but she was breastfeeding her second son right then as she was talking on the phone to me, and the dog, or maybe the cat, just puked on the stairs and it was still all over her sock, not to mention the carpet, and she hadn't had a decent night's sleep since the first son was born and he just started grade one, so don't hold your breath waiting for this novel, she told her agent last week.

"Wait," she said. "Back the fuck up. Do you mean to tell me you can't feel your nipples, like at all? God, what I wouldn't give to not feel his little teeth coming in, day by day by day. I believe this is why babies are born toothless. No one would breastfeed at all if the little fuckers were born with a mouth full of teeth. You have to ease yourself in to excruciating pain like that," she informed me.

I could hear water running in the background and the dog barking.

"Besides, switching nipples is serious fucking business, and anyone who can't see that hasn't had their nipples removed and stitched back on again. Yet. He's young. It's his job to turn on the ones who made him, who fed him, who taught him. It's a rite-of-passage thing. It's in all those fucking parenting books Jin is always bringing home. I tripped over *How to Raise a Feminist* the other day and fully felt like killing him for two days. It's the lack of sleep, I tell him, but some days I suspect I actually do want to kill him.

"Anyways, don't take any of this personal. It's not even really about you, or what you wrote or said, or didn't write or say. It about him flexing his brand-new biceps or spreading his newly feathered wings, or whatever it is the kids do these days to make sure we know that we are officially irrelevant now, and that they invented everything radical. You probably did it to someone too, pal, think back. Next."

She has a way of putting things into perspective. That's why I called her.

FIVE: BY ANY OTHER NAME

I WAS LUCKY, I know, growing up like I did. Weekdays in the summer when my mom couldn't find a free sports camp or Boys and Girls Club outdoor activity, and my grandmother Flo was living in Nanaimo still, and Grandma Pat was up cooking in one of the construction camps or on a trip in her camper with Pearly, her dog, or whatever, and everybody else was busy, I would just go to work in the shop with my dad. It started pretty young, with sweeping and bolt sorting, if I remember right. I will have to ask him.

Sweeping, sweeping, there was always sweeping: aluminum shavings that peeled from the tips of drill bits into razor-sharp silver curlicues, long like phone cords and all over the greasy concrete floor. There was cat litter scattered from dusty bags to soak up spilled oil, and ruby-red transmission fluid and antifreeze and shiny-on-the-inside clumps of dirty bearing grease. Floating bits and slivers of blue foam insulation, busted- off bolts and stripped screws and lost nuts and cotter pins and washers.

And you had better know the difference. You better know a stripped and useless screw from a stainless, irreplaceable last bit off the new antennae on what's his face's boat or trailer or truck that my dad had dropped a week ago and been looking all over for ever since.

My dad was a welder back then, and still is to this day. He's seventy-two and still working. Back then, he had his own big shop, with the bay doors at either end for pulling giant equipment in and through, and squeaking—fuck, what are they called?—hoists, up on tracks in the ceiling for lifting engines and heavy shit out of heavier shit so you can fix it. It's been too long, I guess, since I went to work with my dad, so I'm forgetting the names of things he taught me about.

But I can still tell an inch-and-a-quarter-length, three-quarter-inch head fine thread bolt from a two-inch-long coarse thread one-inch head bolt, and a lock washer from a spacer by sight at a distance, to this day.

I'm calling him right now. It's 6:30 a.m., I'm jet-lagged from my tour in Southeast Asia, and he has already been up for hours. The dude barely sleeps anymore.

It's a chain hoist, he tells me. I'm on the phone with him for an hour. He's trying to learn the internet and wants to figure out how to email me these pictures he took on his iPad of the sauna he is building, but the other old guy who is teaching him the internet went to Germany for Christmas, so it's going to have to wait, unless this lady who works at the corner store he's having over for dinner tonight is some kind of computer wizard too and knows how to work Netflix, he tells me.

He taught me how to drive and weld and measure twice and saw a two-by on a perfect ninety by eye and work the forklift and back up a trailer and make a jig out of scraps and chop kindling and, and. Everything he taught me and all the jobs it got me over the years so I could eat and pay the bills and keep a truck on the road and tour and do shows so I could be a writer one day. It all started with sweeping and sorting the bolts.

Landscaping. First for the city, and then for Jeff at Iditarod. My dad bought me a lawn mower for my sixteenth birthday and told me, "Here, you won't ever have to work for anyone else now if you don't want to." It was a good one too: four-stroke, gas-powered, with a clutch and a drive chain, a shiny red Honda that I paid the rent with more than a dozen times in my early days, for sure.

It was when I was landscaping on the deep mansioned west side of Vancouver in the rain, trying to dig a ditch through the tree roots, that I decided to go to school to be an electrician. A good trade.

I learned wiring from an ex-German-soldier-turned-electrician named Otmar Weltzelmeyer, and how to actually wire stuff from a carpenter named Richard, who hired me to help him build solar houses on small islands off the coast of British Columbia. This turned out to be the best straight job I ever, ever had, but I was too stupid to know it then. I learned more about building and fixing stuff from Richard than I did from any other man in my life, next to my dad, and my uncles Rob and Kevin and John and Fred and Jack.

Then it was the movies. My neighbour Lynn, the lesbian filmmaker, said, "Hey, if you can wire a house, then you can totally be a lamp operator," and she wasn't wrong. I worked hauling cable and lights and gels for a couple of years. And because I could wire stuff, I got hired to build some props for a show called *The New Addams Family*, and then come on set to operate Uncle Fester's light-up lie detector or make Lurch flash green and red when Wednesday made him into a Christmas tree. And that was how I ended up switching over to the props department.

My boss in the props department—hey, I guess I better change her name because of the story I am about to tell about her, but before I start, can I just say there was so much more to Debbie Shore than this shitty story? She was funny and let us all smoke in the props room and worked it out with the production office so that me and Chris, the other props guy, could split the job so both of us got to work forty hours a week, instead of eighty like everybody else. She lived with her ex, the fading rock star, and her new boyfriend, and everybody got along for the kids, and they had a huge house to all share anyways. She was a lot more than what happened in the props room every Thursday afternoon when the paycheques arrived on her desk from the production office upstairs. I don't even know if she knew how much it broke me down every week, and I can't even blame her for that because I didn't even know until years later, looking back on it all.

You get paid once a week in the film industry, on Thursday afternoons around two p.m. Someone from accounting does the rounds of the set, bearing the blessed bundles of cheques elastic-banded into stacks for each department: electrics, grips, carps, greens, craft services, props.

This was back before I changed my name legally. Production was cool with me and put Ivan on the call sheet, so that is what everyone called me. But the accountants were accountants and still had my legal name on all payroll paperwork, so only the people who processed, printed, and passed out the cheques knew my legal name. Enter Debbie Shore.

Looking back, I can't understand what would have possessed her the first time even, and why she would have chosen to repeat this ritual every Thursday for the nearly two years we worked together on fifty-six half-hour episodes that each took four twelve-to-eighteen-hour days to shoot.

Anyhow. I would pop into the props lock-up in the studio to have three drags off of someone's already-lit cigarette while they were tweaking the lights or turning around on set, and Debbie would jump up from her desk with my paycheque in her hand and laugh her too-little-girl-for-her-age laugh and say, "Whose cheque is this? And who are you? Sorry, can you repeat that, [insert deadname here]? And who do we have here, Miss [Deadname]? [Deadname], here you go, now don't spend it all in one place." And so forth. Every week. Every Thursday.

I would cringe. I never laughed back, and she never seemed to notice that I didn't. My gums would tighten around my teeth, my eyelids would ache, my tongue would go dry and scrape at the back of my throat when I tried to swallow around the unnamed ball of squashed-up silence, and I would suck it up and try to smile and stuff the white envelope into my back pocket. It was the most money I had ever made, and everybody knew there was a lineup of probably more qualified props probably guys down at the union hall, waiting to take my job if I didn't like the sound of the name on my paycheque.

I wasn't out at work about being trans. I mean, I looked pretty much how I look now, only younger. And I dressed for the most part how I dress now, only cheaper and more prone to wide-collared vintage polyester shirts. And I had gone by the name Ivan for years already, but I didn't actually use the word "trans," and I hadn't ever had any kind of conversation about pronouns with anyone, even myself. It was 1998, and unless you were a bearded trans man, if you had been assigned female at birth, then your pronoun was she back then. I wouldn't have ever even considered asking to be called anything else, especially at work. It's hard to explain if you weren't around for it, and

I know it's been said a million times, but things really were different back in the day.

I had a kid in Singapore ask me last month how I cope emotionally with being misgendered all the time. They were a thin wisp of a kid, in their first year of college and tender all over, I could tell, tucked into an armchair in the multi-purpose room on campus, wearing a scarf pulled up around their chin and mouth, and hiding wing-like shoulder blades and collarbones under an oversized jean jacket, even in that heat and humidity.

I realized as I was saying it out loud that I am almost impervious now to someone using the wrong pronoun for me. It is an irritant at best, like a black fly behind my ear when I'm trying to put a fishhook on my line, not even a mosquito, and certainly not capable of taking any of my flesh, like a horsefly. I notice it, but it is easily swatted, and crushed. It does not touch me inside in any way, and simply gives me intel on the person who is speaking to or about me. It helps me categorize the speaker, no more, no less: friend, ally, stranger, unhip layperson, oblivious cis, lazy host, or intentional foe. Good to know.

It's hard to see a kid in pain like that. It's important to say the right thing when asked a question like this. But sometimes there really isn't a right thing to say.

What I really wanted this kid to know is that they are going to need to somehow build up the callouses around their heart a little. That they cannot and should not ever give up their power so easily to another, shouldn't put any shred of their own self-worth into the sloppy hands of a stranger, or anyone.

I stumbled through my imperfect answer to that kid, and I know that I prefaced it with a disclaimer, something to the effect of "I can only ever speak for myself ..."

I wish I had told them to stand up full inside themselves and imagine that they are protected by a full suit of shimmering armour made of feathers, made of sequins, made of the six hundred skins they have already shed to become what they are right now in this minute. I wish I had told them to live inside their feathered armourskin with such surety and self-love that who they really are inside could never be shaken by any words stuck to or shot at them from outside of themselves, ever, not ever, no way.

But then I remembered payday in the props lock-up and I knew that they are not ready yet. They are eighteen and unarmoured. I remember how it felt to stand there, swallowing my silence because I didn't know the words for me yet.

I wish I had told that tender kid that there will come a time when all those wrong names and words will bounce and roll off of their back like they do mine now, and they will one day be able to say, "Bring it on, I got this. Call me what you want, you can't touch me, but if you get it right, it will touch me. It's up to you, so you decide." And this will be the truth. Most days.

Some would say I should thank Debbie Shore for teaching me to be tough, but fuck that. I say it's a terrible way to learn anything. And she was more than this tiny, petty, cruel dance she made me do with her on Thursdays, but you know, that is what I remember first, and most, about her now. So you decide what you want me to remember about you because, it's true, I forget almost nothing. It's a strange kind of blessing that I can still hear her words in my head right now, and find the memory so easy on my tongue like it was yesterday, not two decades later.

Oops, I meant to change her name to protect the parts of her that weren't guilty, but I forgot. Her name was Debbie Shore, but let's call her Dianne Small, shall we?

SIX: TO BE CLEAR

I WANT IT said for the record that I don't believe the answer to making the world safer for our youth is teaching queer and trans kids that they need to toughen up to face down this world. They should not have to. A kid shouldn't have to learn to live through trauma and swallow a diet of other people's ignorance simply to become themselves. We need to be changing this world faster. We need to soften this world up, not make our kids harder.

SEVEN: MONTHLY DUES

I HAVE MADE a living writing and performing these last many years, and I haven't had to work a trades job since 2003 or so, when I quit the film business for good after I got that first teaching job up at Capilano, then College now University. That at least covered the rent and then a little back then. It wouldn't now, though, so I know I'm lucky, especially in this goddamn city these days.

I miss physical labour, though, I do. I mean, the road can pound your body, make no mistake: planes and trains and that thing my Achilles does now after thirteen hours of driving, and my back is tweaked permanent too, from hauling gear and merch and suitcases and who knows what else over the years. I know my knees and back are grateful I'm not pulling wire on a construction site or humping dollies of gear up mountainsides on a film set or mowing lawns and digging ditches, but man, I used to sleep good back then, and I loved it when my biceps were hard like apples, and I remember the salt taste of farmer-tan-and-good-work-in-the-hot-sun sweat, not nervous or slept-on-a-plane sweat. And callouses, man, I miss those too. I mean on my palms, not my fingertips from playing guitar, though those are cool as well.

I have days when I dream of quitting the road and getting a job as an electrician again, buying aluminum checker plate tool boxes for the back of my truck and a new hard hat and digging out the old tool belt. I've still got it, and I know exactly where it is right now. I could be ready for work in a couple of minutes, still, to this day.

I know it wouldn't be that easy. I mean, I never saw any fifty-year-old female- assigned trans people, ever, on any of the job sites I was on, in any of the trades I did. I know they're out there somewhere, probably more of them now than ever before. I just don't know any.

My ticket is expired, too, and my union memberships lapsed years ago. IATSE were real bastards about it, to be honest, and repeatedly referred to me as "sister" when they called to say they were taking my name off the register, and no, there was no way to keep my name on any of their lists unless I was paying monthly dues, working or not, writing career or not. I remember that day, in the late fall of 2003, standing outside Continental Coffee on Commercial Drive and telling the woman from the union hall, "Yes, I guess I am saying I'm no longer interested in being in the union. I just can't afford it on my writer's income." That was a hard door, a scary door, to close behind me, but I closed it and never looked back.

I was going to be a writer. I was going to quit the International Alliance of Theatre and Stage Employees and become a member of the Writers' Union of Canada.

The dues are way cheaper, as you would imagine they'd be.

EIGHT: ANALOG

So I'M WRITING this series of essays, starting in 1989, about when I first came out, and looking back over thirty queer years now, and figuring it out in between the lines. And I think to myself, *I wish I still had that Joan Armatrading cassette,* and *I wish I still had any one of the many camper vans I have owned over the years.* I still love that kind of mouldy smell of the sleeping bag that lives on the bed in a camper van. It's how I write; it's how I remember: smell, taste, sounds, and especially music. If I want to write about the summer of 1989, then I'm going to need that album, but on cassette, or maybe the record, something real-time, a hard copy analog physical thing that you have to put on or flip over or rewind and fast-forward. Spotify is great, but it's not the same. I'm also going to need Tuck & Patti's *Love Warriors* and *Pirates* by Rickie Lee Jones and *Blue* by Joni Mitchell.

I bought a pound of coffee, an eighth of indica, and six albums on vinyl at Red Cat Records, and I got to work.

In 1992, when I was twenty-three years old and home in the Yukon working for the summer to make money for school, my buddy Chris Clarke called my parents' landline to tell me that Tuck & Patti were coming to the Bald Eagle Festival in Haines, Alaska, and it was only a five-hour drive and she was going to bring her new canoe and could I bring my tent and the blue cooler? We could take the Subaru, she said; she just got new brakes, finally.

She had a whole plan, and I guess, in retrospect, maybe I should have asked more questions. First of all, Chris was new to tying canoes to the roofs of Subarus, and the boat slid off sideways and also a little bit forward in the wind like a drunk guy's ball cap the first good corner we took on the road just before the junction and the turnoff to Highway 3.

She said we were going to camp at Mosquito Lake and canoe down the Chilkat River into Haines, stash the canoe and walk into town, and then get our friend Lori to pick up the canoe with her truck after the concert and drive us back to the campground. I'm looking at the proposed route on a map on my phone right now as I write this, something I definitely should have done in 1992, before I got into that canoe and pushed off from the shore of that peaceful if buggy Mosquito Lake. Well, obviously not a map on my iPhone back in '92 but a real paper map, of course. You get my drift.

I could tell you all about the salmon and the eagles and the gigantic bear we saw while floating serenely down the Chilkat for most of that day, but the story really picks up when the river began to widen at its mouth and the current smacked up against the force of the frigid waters of the north Pacific Ocean. We hadn't checked the tide tables, either, and the river's determined waters stood up sideways to meet the indifferent and indomitable incoming tide. Icy Alaskan water slopped over the sides of the canoe, and I quickly could not feel the fingers on my hand as it scooped and bailed with the top half of a plastic four-litre milk jug with the blue lid screwed on tight.

Chris was at the stern, being stern. We bailed and paddled into the tide for what seemed like an hour but Chris swore later was only fifteen minutes or so. My shoulders and arms were rubber holding the paddle. The wind picked up. We just weren't moving at all. My feet were soaked and I couldn't feel my toes now, either. I started singing a song and the lyrics went something like, "We're not going anywhere, we're not moving at all," and I could see the shore about a click away, calling to us, but Chris kept steering us straight into the middle of the mouth of the river.

I fixed my eyes on a yellow sign glinting in the conifer green next to the little road that curled alongside the riverbank. The road sign was lined up with the tip of the canoe. I closed my eyes and counted for 100 strokes of my paddle and opened them up again and found the sign again. It was now a couple of canoe lengths in front of us, meaning that even paddling full speed ahead, we were actually going backwards.

Chris caved and stuck her paddle upright in the chuck and swung the nose of the canoe so we were bound for shore. I whooped triumphantly. We were going to stash the canoe and hitchhike into Haines, and I would live long enough to see Tuck & Patti play live in a big field under the midnight sun.

I remember watching them that night, entranced by how much they looked like they loved each other up there, still, after all those years and all those stages. Patti rolling out jokes and anecdotes in her honey-over-gravel voice. I remember her telling this story about waiting tables, just like one of the jobs I was doing that summer, and her words shot possibility into my chest.

She was an artist, but she used to be just like me, I thought. She used to pour coffee and count tips and dream about being something else. She used to dream about getting out of that town for good and being a singer and making people feel things. And here she was. Something else up there on that stage. Something magic. Something real but not really real, at the same time.

In 2012, Chris Clarke called me up in January and said, "Coyote, let's go to Frostbite this year. Come home. Let's go and see some music. Let's get inspired again. Like that summer."

"Okay," I said, "but this time we're driving in a fucking car and parking right outside and walking into the theatre like normal concertgoers."

The night of the concert, Chris and I went over to our friend Brenda's place and ate moose meat stew and drank whiskey and played the ukulele, and it was super fun, even though it was still two years or so before the impending divorce, so things were pretty tense between Brenda and her now ex-wife. I picked up on all the unspoken hidden-by-Christmas- jam-cookies-and-tinsel-still-on-the-tree tension between them right away, because I recognized it from my own home, back in Vancouver.

And then off we went to the theatre. We had flasks full of Jameson and a healthy joint in a Sucrets tin, and we pretty much cried non-stop through the entire show, because it was four different songwriters all trying to sing the saddest songs they knew. But it was a good cry, because tears set to music are almost always the good kind of cry.

Our buddy Michelle Emslie told us after the show that there was going to be a closing party for the whole festival at the Bauer brothers' place and asked us did we want to go?

"The Bauers'?" I asked, one eyebrow raised. "The party bunker?"

I had grown up with Greta Bauer, the only daughter of the Bauer brood. I knew all her brothers: the Bauer boys. They were famous in Whitehorse, the dad too: Old Man Bauer. Werner. More infamous, I guess, with their red-gold curly, curly hair, and how hard it was to tell them apart unless you grew up with them, like I did, and even then, I had to do a double-take sometimes. Andreas smiled more. And Thomas was slightly better looking, like he had the same features as his brothers, but they were just put together a bit different. And Victor was the oldest and scariest somehow, something mean, maybe, in his eyes, but it was hard to say, really, because he talked the least, as I remember.

The Bauers lived in a rambling house in Crestview, a subdivision of Whitehorse, just a little farther north and across the Alaska Highway from Porter Creek, where I grew up. Crestview was less than half a click from the industrial section of Porter Creek, where Hector Lang's compound was, where my dad rented his shop. Greta used to come over to play with me and my sister and Hector's granddaughter Sara and a couple other grubby local kids whose dads were mechanics or welders or autobody guys or crane operators. Her brothers were more elusive, spotted briefly dropping Greta off with their dirt bikes and then disappearing into the pine trees, indistinguishable from each other until you got up close, even though no one wore a helmet back then, hardly ever. The Bauer boys. They were weird, everyone seemed to think. They kept to themselves, they were German, they were dangerous, maybe even, though no one seemed to know exactly why. Their old man hung out at the dump and salvaged old wood and straightened out bent nails and saved them in coffee cans to build additions on their house across the highway.

The Bauer boys had burned that rambling house down a few years ago, but instead of building another house on that giant lot on the hill, they kind of just stitched three trailers together and tacked a giant tin roof onto one side that was held up by four-by-four beams painted with creosote, and the party bunker was born.

Frostbite Music Festival had taken to hiring out the Bauer boys and the party bunker for the festival's closing night festivities so all of their volunteers and staff could have the night off after the last show and celebrate, and someone else would clean up after it was all over.

So Brenda, Chris, and I squeezed into my mom's boyfriend's truck and off we went. I hadn't seen the party bunker before; I had only heard tell of it.

It looked like what it was: three trailers tacked together with kind of an open-walled airplane hangar propped off one side, with a corrugated tin roof covering steel rafters and beams. There was a roaring campfire inside the airplane hangar and a gathering of mismatched couches and nailed-together two-by-ten benches clustered around the crackling flames. It smelled like burning tires. There were three teal portable outhouses lined up just to the right of the front door, a new skiff of fluffy snow on their roofs. *I bet the neighbours just love living next to the party bunker*, I thought, shaking my head a little.

"It's pretty loud in there," I said. "It might get a bit ... Yukon. I'm not sure I'm up for this tonight, not after having my heart torn out by thirty sad songs in a row. When either of you is ready to go, just tug on your earlobe like this, and we can leave right away."

Brenda and Chris both nodded inside their parkas and Sorel boots and woolen mitts with wolf fur trim. They were well bundled, as my mom would say.

The door had a sign on it that said *PLEASE KEEP YOUR BOOTS ON INSIDE*, and the crowd on the other side of it was so huge I had to squeeze the door open wide enough to slide my body sideways into the mash of people inside.

The first trailer held the stage, and a punk band was playing. Orange extension cords fed smoking PAR can lights with orange and red and blue gels clothespinned to them. The lights were clamped and haywired to criss-crossed pipe and two-by-four rafters in the ceiling. People were moshing in their snow boots and parkas on the muddy plywood floor.

The second trailer had pretty much been gutted, except for a bathroom way at the back with an *Out of Order* sign on the door. A row of refrigerators lined one side of the trailer, and a row of avocado and harvest-gold and white electric stoves lined the wall facing the refrigerators. Someone was pulling multiple take-home frozen pizzas out of the ovens with a scorched dish towel. A giant vat of something bubbled on a stove and crusted around the burner, and the sink overflowed with dishes. There were also industrial rubber garbage cans lined with black garbage bags in every available corner.

The third trailer contained multiple couches from the seventies and eighties, and La-Z-Boy chairs bleeding foam stuffing, and the lights were dimmed a little. Every time someone opened the back door to go out into the back yard, a guy who appeared to be fast asleep opened one eye and barked to close the door.

The back yard on the other side of that door contained another had-to-be-illegal-in-the-city-limits bonfire and about 100 more people. The sky was crystal clear and whizzing with one of the most spectacular displays of northern lights I had ever seen in all my years. The sky had shimmered a little here and there on our drive up the highway to Crestview, but now the lights were out in all their green and pink ball gown splendour.

The giant bonfire shot hot air balloons of sparks up into the aurora borealis every time someone threw another log onto it. The punk band pulsed from inside the first trailer, competing with tendrils of "For Those about to Rock (We Salute You)" by AC/DC bleeding out from a pair of speakers propped on the railing of the stairs that led up to the back door of trailer number three.

We all stood around the fire with the northern lights swirling above us, our faces glowing and our asses freezing, stomping to keep our feet warm and sidestepping to keep the smoke out of our eyes when the wind shifted.

Then a guy wearing a red down jacket with duct tape patches finished his beer and smashed the can against his own forehead, which made him stumble backwards a little and knock the guy standing directly behind him on his ass. Knocked-down guy leapt up and charged at beer-can-to-the-head guy, slamming him in the kidneys with two closed fists and catapulting him right into the bonfire. He nimbly leapt through the coals and sparks, and emerged on the opposite side of the fire with only the bottom hem of his jeans aflame. A giant ooh rippled through the crowd, and everyone kicked snow at the flames. Someone kept yelling, "Stop, drop, and roll!" but the guy heeded none of these commands. The pant-leg fire was extinguished in short order, and someone handed him a new beer.

I shook my head again and looked over at Brenda and Chris, who were both tugging on their earlobes repeatedly, signalling time to go, time to go.

I dropped them both off downtown and then pulled into the parking spot behind my mom's condo, the engine of the truck ticking and the heat in the cab quickly giving way to the cold air outside.

A red fox padded from behind the dumpster next to the empty lot next door and sat down under the streetlight, watching me watch it. It licked its lips and picked up its front paws one by one and shook them a little, tipping its ears toward me and coiling the muscles of its back legs to spring when I shifted in my seat.

We both sat like that in the alley for a long while, each of us waiting for the other to move, until the sound of an approaching snowmobile broke the quiet, and the fox loped off and disappeared under the wooden stairs of the shitty apartments, the ones with the peeling paint and the giant penumbra of flattened cigarette butts around the back door.

I tiptoed up the stairs and squeaked across the fresh snow on the deck that led to my mom's back door, slipped out of my boots, hung up my parka, and padded in my wool socks up to the spare room.

I fell asleep that night wondering if I ever wrote a song about my hometown, would it be a love song, or maybe not?

I'm sitting here now in my office, drinking coffee and listening to Joan Armatrading. "Are you for or against us? We are trying to get somewhere," she sings. To me, her music has always been songs of resistance, songs of difference.

I asked my friend Clyde the other day if he had ever heard of her. Maybe one of my first queer heroes.

"Joan who?" he said. "How do I spell it? Should I check her out?"

We are in danger at all times now of forgetting our elders. Forgetting to cry to their songs, and to learn from their words. I realize that I have only myself to blame for this. I haven't handed any newly out baby queers today's equivalent of a Joan Armatrading cassette or a copy of *Stone Butch Blues*. I am supposed to repeat the names Alberta Hunter and Minnie Bruce Pratt and Joan Nestle and Jeanne Córdova and Marsha P. Johnson and Sylvia Rivera and Stormé DeLarverie and Miss Major Griffin-Gracy and the Daughters of Bilitis. I am supposed to whisper those names into the ears of a nineteen-year-old baby butch from rural Manitoba in a dyke bar at the bottom of a flight of piss-smelling stairs that lead to a greasy alley behind a hotel in a big city full of small-town homos looking for each other. I am supposed to especially remember the bull dykes and the trans women and the black and brown queers, because the white gay men who have fallen will have airports named after them, and Hollywood will remember the cleaned-up and sterilized versions of their stories, but the remembering of the rest of us will still be up to the rest of us. I am supposed to be the bridge, and somehow, I have forgotten this.

But I can't whisper history into younger ears in the dyke bar because the dyke bars are all gone now. I have no idea where the young queers are gathering. I guess I could go and ask around on Instagram.

And I will pick up my pen and remember to remember.

NINE: UNBECOMING

I WAS NEVER really all that pretty. I pretty much knew that my whole life. Not pretty. Good at other stuff, though, I would tell myself way back, when it seemed like the most important thing a girl could be was pretty. When I was nineteen years old, in 1988, a girl kissed me on Friday the 13th, and I realized maybe I was something else, not pretty, but still, maybe something. Then I switched to trying on handsome. I'm not pretty, but I could be handsome. Maybe that would feel less ugly, I thought.

So now it's thirty years later and I see my friend on Instagram, and they are transitioning, a little more each day, with each bathroom-mirror selfie. But more importantly, this morning they changed their lipstick colour dramatically, going from an everyday no-nonsense red to a delicious dark purple, with an even darker, most immaculate liner, under very bold eyeshadow too, and the lashes, I mean, they had really applied themself, and they looked ... divine.

I was so inspired, I remembered to moisturize.

Several months ago, my friend David A. Robertson began to grow his hair. Like, I'm talking the man now has some luscious hair. He's Cree and over six feet tall and has fathered five children even though he's a vegan, so I'm well aware that I'm not ever going to sport a virile mane like David A. Robertson's, but—

I'm turning fifty years old and suffice it to say I am capable of growing a lot more hair than a lot of dudes my age. In fact, my trans buddy around my age (which can now mean ten years younger than me—I think he's forty-one) even said to me once, several years back, after I had just had another every-three-weeks, millimetre-long barbershop fade, "Man, if I still had any hair, I would grow Justin Bieber hair, dude. That shit would be in my eyes. I would learn to flick my bangs. I swear, maybe a topknot. Whatever, I'd grow it."

So I started growing my hair out, about two months ago now.

There is a line at the end of a story I wrote called "Shouldn't I Feel Pretty" that goes, "I am lucky I can now afford a well-cut shirt and a real silk tie and a fancy jacket with those cool elbow patches and a good haircut once a month ..."

I was in Tokyo last month, day two of my Asia tour, and the first hand that shot up belonged to this young woman from Laos, who was just learning Japanese, and English. I heard later at lunch from her teacher that she was a real thinker, a rebel, a writer, a philosopher.

She said: "You have not had a good haircut in over one month. That part is not true."

And everybody cracked up. She then told me, in English, and with some help from the translator, that I was like a Buddhist story she had studied about a sunflower that once grew very tall but did not bloom or flower, or thus make seeds, but in the end was still beautiful, just in a different way from all the other more common but gloriously blooming and seeding sunflowers. Her name was Aelan and I sent her a message via her prof that my nickname for her was now Sunflower Girl, and she responded that she loves this nickname and is keeping it. Or so says the translator.

Anyway. This morning I saw that picture of the dark purple lipstick, and I thought of all the lipstick I have loved, in all of its many ways. On their lips. On his lips. On my sweetheart's lips. Her lipstick on my cheek on my neck on my chest on her fingertips on the light switch on the doorframe—she smoothes it with her fingers and then touches stuff—on the coffee cup on the spoon on the sheets on the pillowcase. Two kinds of lipstick in her Christmas stocking. On a cigarette butt she tucked into the pocket of my jacket she borrowed that night. Lady Danger Pink Pigeon A Dozen Carnations. On her teeth. On my teeth.

I have loved lipstick all my life, but I have never learned to love it on my own lips, except for on Halloween: a zombie, a vampire, and once, when I was thirteen, a fancy lady. Even at thirteen, I knew that pretending to be a woman was going to be a costume for me.

But I've been changing. Uncovering. Unwrapping myself lately.

Returning. Undoing. Unbecoming. Shedding. Shed. My new middle name is Shed. I changed it, finally, five years ago, and my legal middle name is now Shed. As in, get rid of, or a place to store or do or build, and inspired by Out-in-the-Shed, the character from Tom Spanbauer's book *The Man Who Fell in Love with the Moon*. Shed for short.

I hated my old surname, the one I shed. Unbecoming.

I fought pretty all my life. I bucked the dresses and ribbons and pink, the ladylike and demure and quiet and polite and graceful. I fought makeup and frills. I fought lipstick. For myself, anyway. I was going to be something else—not better, just different.

But it turns out the gender binary fucks us coming, and going.

There is a different kind of masculinity in Tokyo. I had read about it but never seen it with my own eyes. It's an urbane one, a stylish one, a matching-shoes-and-belt-and-cheekbones kind of masculinity. A not-so-much-about-chest-hair-and-beards-and-axes-and-plaid-shirts-on-horseback-with-a-ten-gallon-hat-fifties-cigarette-ad kind of masculinity, like we foster in the West. A kind of masculinity easier for me to exist in. I realized it on about day two of my trip to Asia. I felt like I fit in to this kind of masculinity without having to try so hard, if fitting in was even what I wanted.

Sliding through a crowd as a male-appearing individual is sometimes largely about safety for me, still. But safety aside, I just ... fit better. I didn't have to drop my voice as much. The edges of the gender box marked male were somehow closer to my comfortable reach. I cannot describe it any better than that.

Then I flew from Tokyo to Hong Kong.

I was a guest of the Hong Kong writers festival, and the main venue was an arts centre that used to be a prison. It was a giant square brick place with echoing marble staircases and a cobblestone courtyard in the middle. As I walked through the complex to the gallery where my gig was, I imagined maybe where the exercise yard used to be, or maybe where the gallows once stood. Now it hosts coffee shops and potted shrubs and a poetry slam.

I was to read and answer questions with a trans man from Australia, and our host was a trans woman from the Philippines who now lives in Hong Kong. She is a psychologist and a university professor who was recently arrested by Chinese police for being in a women's washroom. Her case is well known in Hong Kong.

I had repeatedly asked festival folks and Canadian embassy staff how safe I was, or should feel, in public bathrooms in Hong Kong, and nobody seemed to really be able to answer me fully, so I just made sure to pee in my private hotel room bathroom before I went anywhere, and then waited until I got back to the hotel, thus avoiding having to find out personally. They don't cover this material much in the *Lonely Planet* travel guides, and it's hard to find accurate info online. It's always harder for trans feminine people, too, because of the transmisogyny and fearmongering that the alt-right and the TERF army team up to proliferate, and I keep this in mind, while still doing whatever possible to suck it up and go to work and put all the what-ifs out of my mind.

There were two young and beautiful queer people sitting front row and centre at the gig, and I immediately felt a warm puddle of gratitude for their presence in this very straight space that was painted stark gallery white and made of concrete and echoes. They were like two flowers, stretching impossibly to make space for their tenacious stems between cracks in the crumbling sidewalk.

One was wearing a jean vest over a bright white T-shirt with the sleeves rolled up over their biceps, and the other had a nearly shaved head and a paisley button-down under a sensible grey cardigan. My people. We exchanged eye contact and tears, and they both nodded and at one point hugged each other during my reading. We three shared a giant hug after the show. My non-binary family. I felt strangely and suddenly at home inside our embrace, even on the other side of the planet.

Vincy and Rachel. We are friends on social media now, and a little in real life, too, I think. Vincy is a singer and a performer, Rachel a fantastic artist and illustrator.

I felt changed when I got home, inspired by both of them somehow. Vincy and their impeccable eyeshadow. Rachel and their hand-drawn cartoons and carefully lettered poetry. Both of their refusals to be squeezed into any kind of a gender box, shrugging off easy labels and questioning all definitions.

When I first get out of the shower, my bangs now touch my chin. I comb them back with pomade, but by the end of the day, they have escaped and hang into my eyes. I have had to relearn how to flick my hair away from my face, a skill I had forgotten, a skill I left behind me when I was nineteen and cut all my hair off when I first came out.

I'm trying to love my hips.

I've been flipping the word "butch" over in my pocket, considering it in new ways I never did before. Deciding whether I still need it like I used to. Pondering hanging it up in my closet next to a jacket I've grown out of but still keep because of the memories it holds in its seams, in its threads. The smell of it.

I bought some mascara, but I haven't used it yet. I'm experimenting with so-called feminine versions of male-coded clothing. I finally found a pink plaid shirt.

I'm considering a manicure. Yeah, I think I need a camo-print manicure.

I'm unbecoming.

TEN: WHEN I WAS TWENTY-THREE

I STILL THOUGHT that if I just sat down with women who were trans-exclusionary radical feminists, and we could just have a really good talk about everything, they would for sure just come around and see that we are all just in this thing together. I thought a little light bulb would flicker on inside of their hurt and battered hearts, and they would suddenly see all of their sisters standing beside them. I thought they could be talked into the truth, and we could then begin to work together to make the world a better place for all women. When I was twenty-three I actually believed that.

When I was twenty-three I never spent a minute of any day hating my own body. Except for my tits, but they were so small back then, I could almost just ignore them.

When I was twenty-three I always trusted that I was going to get the rent together on time for the first of the month. Even when it was already the third of the month. Even when I had to choose between buying ramen noodles and taking the bus.

When I was twenty-three I still thought East Vancouver was an affordable place to live.

When I was twenty-three East Vancouver still was.

When I was twenty-three, and mostly broke most of the time, I considered store- bought tampons kind of a luxury item. A punk rock slam poet from San Francisco taught me how to roll my own tampons from toilet paper pilfered from library and hotel lobby bathrooms. I still think of her whenever I buy a giant box of 100 tampons at Costco.

Sometimes I worry that I will forget her when menopause finally sets into this body permanently.

When I was twenty-three I didn't mind that every pair of footwear I owned and every shirt in my closet were way too big for me. I was used to it.

When I was twenty-three I thought I could just run away from those memories.

When I was twenty-three I thought smoking looked cool, not sad.

When I was twenty-three I would do the math about how old I would be in the year 2000. Thirty-one. *We will have found the cure for AIDS by then*, I remember thinking.

When I was twenty-three I only had two tattoos. One of those tattoos is now buried under the ink of a newer one, and the other is a blurry smudge on my right shoulder. A pink triangle.

When I was twenty-three I kept a journal. I wrote or drew or glued stuff into it nearly every day. The big black, unlined art books that you used to be able to buy at East Side Datagraphics on Commercial Drive. I would splurge on a new one every new year, and scrabble in December to fill the pages of the old one so they didn't go to waste. I wrote most of my stories that eventually appeared in the book *Boys Like Her* longhand in those journals. I would drag them around in my backpack and memorize my stuff from them backstage before I did open-mic gigs and cabaret nights in venues that have now all burned down or been torn down: the Glass Slipper, the Mighty Niagara, that place on the Drive right by Venables. I can't remember its name. I can't believe I forget the name of that place. Electric something something?

That's the thing about forgetting. I used to think I would only forget the stuff that didn't really matter. But that is not what happens at all. You just forget. An old man warned me of that one time, when I was about twenty-three. I forget his name now.

When I was twenty-three I thought the number 23 held a certain kind of magic. I still do.

When I was twenty-three I experienced my first real heartbreak. The kind that catches and grows in your throat. The kind that leaks out of your eyes on the bus. The kind of broken heart that feels bottomless. The kind that glues your heavy head to your pillow. Makes you forget to eat. We found each other as friends, finally, many years later, at a funeral. Every once in a while she turns her head just so, and it flicks a string inside of me, still wound tight somewhere way inside my chest. Like an echo, like a stain, like an E minor chord sung in a staircase while alone.

When I was twenty-three I still thought that if we could just talk to white supremacists, and people who hate trans people, and misogynists, if we just took the time to love them and have compassion and listen to their pain and tell them a different story about the truth of the rest of us, they would see. They would see us and join us, because isn't love greater than hate? Deep down doesn't every heart just want to beat next to another?

Last night I heard a poet say that love is not a blanket but a cloud. Her name is Juliane Okot Bitek, and I heard her say that last night, and I am fifty years old, and it did not bring me comfort, but it did flick a string inside of me. Like an echo, like a broken heart still pumping blood into my fingertips, like an E chord sung in the underground parking lot of a condominium they built where I used to gather and tell stories to other twenty-three-year-olds wearing third-hand boots way too big for them.

It's a full moon tonight. A pink moon, they say. I think I'm getting my period. I'm almost done with bleeding. I don't even really need a tampon anymore. Every period now threatens to be my last.

I will not miss it.

ELEVEN: 237 WORDS

I'VE BEEN PLANNING this series of essays in my head, in the shower or halfway through walking the dog or peeling the yams for supper, reaching around in the back of my head, into the ether, to find the tendrils of thought that need to be pulled and pushed together somehow.

First, I have to make a coffee and take a shower and clean the house and put on a record. I can still write if I don't do these things, but if I do them intentionally, it calls the words to me quicker and better, and all I have to do is be ready to catch them.

It's January 1, 2019, at 2:53 p.m., and I am home in Whitehorse, typing at my mom's kitchen table. I am meant to be writing about mentorship and role models and forgiveness and call-out culture and how cruel queer and trans people can be to each other, but I just got back from walking around Long Lake in the pink and lavender fading hours of a Yukon deep-winter day with the little dog and my sweetheart and my aunt Roberta, who never has a mean word to say about anyone, like, ever, and big-city capital LGBTQ community politics seem too far away to capture accurately, and it feels a shame to even conjure them up right now, just to get my word count done today.

Two hundred and thirty-seven.

TWELVE: REMEMBER THAT SONG

I WANT TO talk about "Walk on the Wild Side" by Lou Reed. I want to talk about that song.

My uncle Rob was a car salesman, so he always had a new set of wheels when I was a kid, and the first time I ever heard that song I was in his shiny new truck and we were pulling a boat out to Fox Lake in the Yukon to go fishing and camping for the weekend, and it's funny how a song can do that, how it can reach right through the speakers in the dusty truck door next to your twitching twelve-year-old thigh, and you just know that listening to the words is going to change you somehow, and the words haven't even started. It was just that bassline at the beginning, but I already knew.

I was riveted by the time the chorus of doo de doos came. There I was, a twelve-year-old trans kid with no words for who I was and no picture in my head that looked anything at all like who I ever thought I was going to be, until Lou Reed sang those words about Jackie thinking she was James Dean right to me that day. I felt those words enter my ears and slip into my blood, and that blood found its way into my heart to make it pound and drink in oxygen, and all of a sudden someone else like me existed in the world. In that moment, a lonely kid split and became the possibility that there were at least two of us, plus Candy and Holly and Little Joe and the Sugar Plum Fairy, and, hey, now there was a gang of us, I thought. I just had to one day get to New York City.

Or maybe Edmonton or Toronto. Someplace a bit more believable. I had a great- grandmother in Saskatoon.

Wikipedia says: "'Walk on the Wild Side' is a song by Lou Reed from his second solo album, *Transformer* (1972). It was produced by David Bowie and Mick Ronson, and released as a double A-side with 'Perfect Day.' The song received wide radio coverage, despite its touching on taboo topics such as transsexual people, drugs, male prostitution, and oral sex."

Even Johnny Cash growling out "A Boy Named Sue" made me feel like I was possible, like I could maybe grow up and still exist. But Jackie was so much closer to the truth of me.

Then came that song "Lola" by the Kinks. I think I first heard it while stoned on hash in Stacey Henley's weird little cabin out behind his parents' house, sitting at the kitchen table with my snow boots still on and my parka hanging on the back of the chair. It was grade ten and I was trapped inside a bad perm and blue eyeshadow, like so many of us were back then.

High school was a rough time for me. In retrospect, I was desperately trying on womanhood, and failing most days. When applying makeup and getting dressed, I was very conscious that I was a fraud, and certain inside that everyone around me knew it.

"Listen to this next bit. Shhhhh." Ted Whitney was standing next to the record player, one hand held up in front of him, head tilted toward the speakers. "Listen to the words. This song rules."

We listened to that song probably about ten times in a row, figuring out the lyrics, what it all meant. I don't remember anyone uttering the word "fag." I have no recollection of that at all. What I do remember is all of us agreeing that the Kinks did, in fact, rock.

We all went to see the midnight screening of *The Rocky Horror Picture Show*, too, and threw rice and held newspapers over our heads and sang along. Nobody in the car ride home after said a word about Frankenfurter, or the fishnets, not even the boys, which seems strange to me now, as they were all so quick to claim that any perceived slight against anything but simple, starkly defined masculinity was gay, and gay was only ever a very, very bad thing to be.

Then came *Purple Rain*. The song, the album, the movie. Prince and his outfits. A bunch of working-class kids in the Yukon wearing nothing more adventurous than white Reeboks and painters' pants and jean vests never batted an eye at Prince's wardrobe.

And then there was Bowie. And Boy George.

The gendered rules between us were fixed and fast and unquestioned. Unless you were a male rock star. Twisted Sister could wear spandex pants. Everyone had that Bowie poster taped up on the back of their bedroom door. Everyone dressed up like Kiss for Halloween. It was all okay if you sang or played electric guitar.

Unless you were k.d. lang. Now that was some weird dykey shit coming out of Alberta.

I graduated from high school wearing a sea-foam satin dress and nylons with a little sparkle in them. I had long curly hair with baby's breath flowers in it. My mom kept telling me I looked lovely. I look okay in the photos, but not so much in the video. In the video

I walk across the stage to get my diploma like I'm wearing work boots, not dyed-to-match pumps.

My grandmother Pat confessed to me a few years later that I looked like a dog at the park with a cone on its head in my graduation dress. "You walked like a trucker. You still do," she told me.

A couple of years ago, I watched a drama unfold on Facebook, and then in the media, about a campus event at a university in Ontario. The student society had issued a public apology for including the song "Walk on the Wild Side" on a playlist.

"It's come to our attention that the playlist we had on during bus pass distribution on Thursday contained a song with transphobic lyrics," said a portion of the post. "We now know the lyrics to this song are hurtful to our friends in the trans community and we'd like to unreservedly apologize for this error in judgment."

A couple of days later, the same student society issued a sort of apology for their first apology: "We recognize Lou Reed's involvement in and contributions to the LGBTQ+ community, and regret that our post was perceived by some to mean otherwise. We appreciate Lou Reed as an artist, and did not speak to his character in our post," the group said. "Our sole intent was to acknowledge that the lyrics, in current day, are now being consumed in a different societal context."

For some reason, this non-controversy erupted into an international mainstream media news debacle, with conservative pundits and aging music critics as far away as the UK claiming this was yet another sign of political correctness taken to the extreme, and free speech being rampantly trodden in kids these days' rabid quest to not offend anyone.

Even though the student society claimed to have issued the initial statement of their own accord, and not as a result of anyone, trans or not, complaining about the lyrics to the song.

This is what I see, two years later, combing through the mainstream media accounts of the controversy that never really happened: I see young students questioning pop culture in a way I don't remember ever doing when I was eighteen years old, and trying to be considerate of others who are more marginalized than they are. I see them not being afraid to step up and apologize if they are concerned that their actions have caused harm, and then apologizing again and clarifying their intentions, and holding themselves accountable for their words and actions.

The only people I saw actually getting offended by any of it were the journalists themselves, complaining about students complaining about things that nobody can provide proof anyone ever complained about. A completely fabricated flap that probably got a lot of clicks from budding incels and angry fans of a certain tenured psychology professor at the University of Toronto.

I wonder now how many of those probably mostly volunteer student society members came back for more of that thankless shit and abuse the following year? "We eat our leaders," my friend Bet once told me, and she seems to get righter and righter every year I manage to get older.

Of course those lyrics read differently today than they would have in 1972, when Lou Reed first released that song. I can't even bear to read parts of a book I published in 2010 now, because it is today. Because I am fifty now, not forty-one, and everything is so different. I am trying not to wonder what a sixty-year-old me will have to say about these words one day, too, so that I can even continue to keep typing them.

In ten years there will be another shiny crop of eighteen-year-old queers on a campus somewhere, dissecting today's pop songs and literary dinosaurs, discarding what doesn't apply anymore and debating what remains.

As it should be.

10. TO AND FROM

DEAR SIR: THANK you for your letter, and for your feedback. I do feel it is important for me to let you know, though, that I suspect that your son is not gay because he read my gay book. I'm pretty sure your son read a gay book because he was already gay. I will pray for both of you as well.

Hello Ivan:

I am a teacher in Coquitlam. This September, I am going to use your "Dear Lady in the Women's Washroom" in my class. I have some questions. Do you mind if I ask you? I am struggling to find resources to back this experience up.

First of all, would you classify this piece as an open letter? Also, do you recommend any charts or evidence-based statistical reports that I can have on hand in case I have some students that bring fear-based rhetoric to the discussion? Or any online videos of your performance work that would support this piece (or "Saturdays and Cowboy Hats," which I will also be using).

Also, I would like to say thank you for your writing. It is very moving and important work.

Regards,

Ms Endicott

Dear Ms Endicott:

Thank you so much for your email, and thank you for including some of my work in your curriculum. I think discussing important social issues in the classroom is an important tool to teach critical thinking, which is a cornerstone of a healthy democracy. And as a queer and trans person who grew up in the Yukon in the seventies and eighties, I know I suffered as a kid from a complete lack of any kind of positive representation or role models that even vaguely resembled me. I am more than happy that you are using my work as a tool to bring both of these vital elements into your students' lives.

Let's begin with the first story of mine, "Dear Lady in the Women's Washroom." I am very aware that the issue of trans people accessing public washrooms is a hot-button topic, and I think it is wise to anticipate that some of your students will bring in some of the fear and misinformation that currently circulates in our courtrooms, political arenas, and media. It is, as you suggest, important to counter this with evidence and the real statistics. I have taken some time to gather some numbers for you. Bear with me here, as I am about to get mathematical.

Up to sixty percent of the human adult body is made up of water, and every living cell in the body needs water to keep functioning. Water acts as a lubricant for our joints, regulates our body temperature through sweating and respiration, and helps to flush waste. We lose water when we sweat, go to the bathroom, and even exhale. If that lost water is not replaced, the total volume of body fluid can fall quickly, and most dangerously, blood volume may drop. Serious dehydration is a medical emergency, and if not reversed, will lead to death.

I am a travelling performer and storyteller. This involves a lot of public speaking and airplane rides, both of which are known to contribute to dehydration. It's a thirsty business, this. I drink a lot of water.

Urinary frequency is vital to health. A healthy person may urinate four to ten times a day. I'm turning fifty this August, so let's go with ten times a day, shall we?—for the sake of easy math, not including the four times I have to get up during the night now, amirite?

My work schedule the last few years involves me being away from home an average of 220 days out of the calendar year, so, excluding the four times I go in the night, because those happen mostly in private hotel bathrooms, let's estimate that when travelling for work, I need to access public bathrooms an average of ten times a day, multiplied by 220 days out of the year, which is 2,200 times annually that I will need to pee in a theatre, university, library, airport, ferry, cultural centre, or, most terrifying, public school bathroom. I try to stay hydrated when not travelling as well, and I try to do things like go to the gym and buy groceries and go to the movies, so let's say I use a public bathroom twice a day on the remaining 145 days I am home, for a combined total of 2,490 public bathroom breaks per calendar year, give or take.

According to a 2013 research paper entitled "Gendered Restrooms and Minority Stress," fifty-four percent or trans people who responded reported adverse health effects from trying to avoid public washrooms, such as kidney and urinary tract infections, and fifty-eight percent reported that they have at times avoided going out in public because of a lack of safe facilities. As a full-time travelling artist, I don't have the option of avoiding public places.

One hundred percent of the time I enter a "ladies'" room, I get nervous about being confronted by a woman who feels I do not belong there. I would estimate this happens, to varying degrees, about thirty percent of the time I choose to brave the ladies' room, which I only do now about twenty percent of my total bathroom visits, because of fifty years of hassles in there. Of this thirty percent when I am confronted or questioned, I would say the vast majority of interactions are relatively harmless: stares, second looks, elbowing of companions, passive-ag-gressive throat clearing, or emphatic door-sign checking. Only about ten percent of these negative exchanges involve gasping, screaming, or other visual fear responses; running out the door; or calling security on me. Only a very small percentage of these incidents include me being struck by a purse or shopping bag or cardboard poster tube, or, once at the beach, a hot-pink Styrofoam pool noodle (true story), which didn't hurt physically but felt personally humiliating for reasons I find difficult to document statistically. Only once have I ever been bruised by a particularly heavy handbag, and only three times have I been physically hauled out of the ladies' room by security guards, and only during one of those three forcible removals did I not have my pants pulled up all the way. Sadly, this was the one time it happened in a major thoroughfare of the Minneapolis airport. One hundred percent of the security guards who have forcibly removed me from women's bathrooms have been decidedly male.

One hundred percent of the time I decide to go to the men's room I also feel nervous, though for different reasons, even though I estimate that 99.9 per cent of the time no men even make eye contact with me in there, and 100 percent of the time I use a stall. In the interest of solid research, though, I should mention that I can't actually be assured that one hundred percent of the people who use the men's room are, in fact, men, as, in order to not draw unnecessary attention to myself in there, I also do not make eye contact with anyone. Only three times have I been aware of possibly being cruised by someone who may or may not have been a man—hard to tell, because I wasn't really looking. Only once has a man spoken to me in the men's room. I was initially so terrified by this interaction that the elderly gentleman who addressed me was forced to repeat his words, which were, and I quote: "Son, do up your shoelace or you will trip and break your neck."

I estimate that I can only find and access a gender-neutral public washroom about fifteen percent of the time, and I am questioned about using the wheelchair-accessible washroom while not appearing to require it about two percent of the time I am entering or leaving one.

Seventy-five percent of the times I am invited to speak about trans issues in a public building, there are no gender-neutral facilities on site for me to use. I find this ironic one hundred percent of the time. As of very recently, about half the time I am invited to speak about bathrooms in a venue with no bathrooms for me, someone has printed up a new sign on a piece of paper and taped it over the gendered signs on the gendered bathrooms, declaring them both now absolutely welcome to all. Only about five percent of these times have these temporary signs been torn down, by what I can only hope is a very small percentage of the public that simply cannot tolerate a bathroom being temporarily gender neutral for the two hours I am on campus.

All of this tends to make me a little nervous, which, of course, makes me have to pee.

Let's move on to support materials and evidence-based data for the second story you asked about, "Saturdays and Cowboy Hats." This story is essentially about me meeting a young tomboy who reminds me of my younger self, or more importantly, her meeting me, someone she could imagine being one day. She is full of questions, such as where did I get my wallet chain, haircut, work boots in my correct size, and that cowboy hat. I like to think this story shines a light on issues of queer and gender-nonconforming representation in an accessible way, using the power of personal narrative to connect the reader to their own memories of childhood loneliness and alienation, and, to use a term popular with the right wing, recruit.

This story I am finding a little harder to quantify. I can find no data to support the need for positive representation and support for queer and/or trans or gender-nonconforming youth that doesn't lead me directly to statistics on suicide or self-harm.

As I am still alive, and relatively sound in body and mind, I will tell you that my methodology seems to have worked for me so far.

I'm pretty sure I spent the first eighteen years of my life convinced I was the only person like me in the whole world: I am one hundred percent certain that having access to any story, song, movie, or sonnet that mentioned the possibility of anything resembling a healthy and happy queer or trans person would have made my childhood easier to navigate, and I come from a very supportive family, especially relatively speaking, no pun intended.

My quality of life improved by one hundred percent immediately after I came out and met other queer people, whether they resembled me in any tangible way outside of their sexuality. Things got significantly better after I first picked up a book called *Stone Butch Blues* by Leslie Feinberg. Even though the story was set in the fifties on the blue-collar side of a very urban American city, I found echoes of myself and much comfort there. I remain convinced that book saved my life. I went on to scour libraries and movie theatres and the streets for positive depictions of butch and trans people and their stories. I then began to write my own. Many of the stories I have encountered that truly represented people I could identify with that weren't built on stereotypes or depict two-dimensional butches aping toxic masculinity appeared in books that I found necessary to write myself. And some of my books need a good solid update to remain with the times. I continue to write myself down to find myself, and so that others like me may find themselves a little, too, and be followed.

I never struggled with math in school. It has always come easily to me. I always got pretty much straight As. Schoolwork was never the problem. School was.

I am one hundred percent grateful that you will be bringing my voice and some of my life into your classroom this September. Ninety-five percent of me is honoured that out of the now-blossoming and ever-increasing body of works by queer and trans artists and performers out there these days, you have chosen to include two of my stories. The other five percent of me allows myself to feel frustrated that my life and experience are not considered enough evidence of my right to thrive and be welcome in public places, and that the very fact of my existence is still considered a topic open to debate. But I know that it is one hundred percent true that my frustration and anger are not the perfect tools for teaching, and my patience and humour are. I have always found the heart to be more powerful than any pie chart.

I remain one hundred percent convinced that the ten percent of your students who are now or will one day identify in some way as queer or trans or Two-Spirit need both of us to bring our best selves to this discussion, because all of those kids really need to leave this world's fear-based rhetoric at the door and truly listen.

I hope these statistics are of some assistance, and I hope my stories help even more. I remain always grateful for good teachers and the work you do to change the world, every day. Well, except those glorious days in July and August, which you totally deserve off.

Thank you for writing.

Note: I wrote this piece in 2017, jet-lagged in a king-sized hotel room bed in Auckland, New Zealand, and delivered it at the Sydney Writers' Festival in Australia a couple of days later. I had just found out from my itinerary that I was expected to deliver a forty-minute lecture "on diversity" to what turned out to be about 600 mostly straight, white festivalgoers. The first question from the audience after I was finished was "When did you have your penis removed?"

I WAS BORN and raised in the Yukon, in northern Canada. I'm pretty much as far away from home as I can get right now. If I travelled any farther away from home at this point, the scales would tip and I would actually be moving closer to where I belong. I was conceived under the northern lights—it's a long story involving a work camp and a conjugal trailer, and my eighteen- and nineteen-year-old parents-to-be—but anyway, I was conceived under the northern lights, the aurora borealis, and where I come from, this is considered by many to mean that I will live an extremely lucky life. So far, I believe that to be true.

One of the hardest things for me about living in a city is that I hardly ever get to chop wood anymore. I am very tidy and I like to cook. I play the baritone saxophone, and I like little dogs and cross-stitching and weightlifting. My favourite colour is robin's-egg blue. I own over 100 neckties. I have inherited from my dad's side of the family a nearly eerie skill for math and numbers, which I rarely use. I chose to be an artist, a writer, and a storyteller. My eleventh book was released last October. I travel for work a lot. Strangers on airplanes unfortunately find me very easy to talk to.

I am a trans person. I have been scheduled to come here today and speak to you about diversity because I am a trans person, but it is important to me that you know those other things about me too.

I'm not an academic. I was eleven years old the first time I remember dreaming of being a writer, and when I was nineteen, my heart confirmed that writing was what I was meant to do, so needless to say, I immediately enrolled in trade school to study to be an electrician. My giant Irish Catholic and Roma family is full of great storytellers and writers, and voracious readers and thinkers, mostly disguised as plumbers and telephone operators and car salesmen. Paying tuition for years to become a writer was simply just not on my radar at that time. I was not connected in any way to anyone who had ever done such a thing.

I was one of two female-assigned humans in a sea of 650 men in the electrical trades department at the British Columbia Institute of Technology. This was not unusual for me. I was the only girl playing in the boys' minor hockey league for eleven years as a youngster, too. I was used to being the only one, or almost the only one.

I'm not sure if I am the only trans person speaking at this festival. These kinds of statistics are rarely kept, and if they are kept, they are not shared with me. It's usually safe for me to assume that I will be the only trans person at the festival, on the panel, in the lineup. I've said it over and over again, and I will say it again right now, I do not and cannot speak for all trans people—I can only ever speak for myself—but some days it is difficult not to feel like that is what is being asked of me.

Being trans is a part of me, and of course it informs how I view my place in the world, and I'm well aware of the fact that it is THE thing about me for some people, but for me it's just one of the things that I am. I'm a Yukoner. I'm a fan of Scandinavian crime novels. I can only eat bananas if they are still a little bit green. I'm ambidextrous. Is that a metaphor, or maybe foreshadowing? I'm also a storyteller.

So, let me tell you a little story.

Last fall I was on tour with my new book, and I was invited to a small literary festival in a pretty white-bread hamlet in Ontario, a couple hours outside Toronto. The kind of town that hosts an apple cider festival in the summer and is bordered by cornfields and pumpkin patches.

A couple of days before my event, the festival tweeted a link to ticket-buying info for my show, with a caption that read: "Ivan Coyote is coming to talk about diversity."

I panicked a little in the airport departure lounge and immediately scanned through my emails from the festival. I thought I was just doing a reading, not any kind of workshop or keynote. I thought maybe I had missed something. I messaged the unknown tweeter from the festival, asking them if I had got my wires crossed somewhere. I was just doing a performance, right? Why had they tweeted that I was talking about diversity? I hadn't prepared anything for that, I wrote, and my event was two days away.

"Oh, sorry," he wrote me back. "I didn't mean to worry you. It's just a new marketing thing we're working on. Yes," he reassured me, "you are just doing a performance, but you know, every time you get up onstage you're kind of talking about diversity, right?"

Silly me. And here all along I thought I was just talking about my life, my reality.

So, here's the rub. Straight white male authors get to write about what they write about. They get to answer questions from journalists about the things that they write about. They get to be on panels talking about the things that they write about, and they get to be experts on the things that they research and think and write about. Nobody ever asks them to be a spokesman for all straight white men all over the world. The rest of us are expected to write about who we are. We can write about other things, but we will always be asked to comment on what it is like to be a woman who writes about politics, or a woman who writes male characters, or a person of colour who writes about medicine or feminism or war, or a queer person who writes about professional football, or a trans person who writes about their family. We are always expected to have wise, compassionate, and patient answers to any kind of question about who we are, in addition to what we write about. Most of the shit we get on Twitter about what we write about has nothing to do with what we wrote and everything to do with who we are. If you don't believe me, then follow Laverne Cox or Roxane Gay or Wanda Sykes or Chelsea Manning and witness it for yourself.

And if you are even thinking about tweeting any of these lines, please, for the love of everything sacred, speak to me afterward and double-check that you have quoted me correctly.

I guess what I am really saying is I will continue to talk about being a non-binary person in a very gendered world until the beautiful, shiny day when people are only interested in my opinions or my characters or my prose and cease to wonder about my genitals or what my parents think about all of this or where I am going to pee after this event is over and how they feel about peeing in the stall right next to me.

What a sweet, sweet day that will be.

And here comes my caveat, okay, and I really do mean it. Some of my closest friends are straight white men. For reals. One of my favourite people in the world is my 350-pound, red-bearded, ham-handed, heavily tattooed heterosexual cousin Dan. He's more like my brother than my cousin. I'm not a man-hater, not by any stretch.

I do hate the patriarchy, though, and I'm not afraid to use terms like "rape culture" and "toxic masculinity" and "cissexism" and "white supremacy," and "genocide."

But I also don't believe that we will fix any of these things by excluding from the conversation those who benefit most from the world's unbalanced power structures. In fact, because so much of the time I am mistaken by much of the world for a straight, white, middle-class man, I believe that it is my obligation to engage with these guys, because in the right light I look just like one of them. I sometimes am allowed fleeting grasps at male privilege, and I also know what it feels like to have those privileges revoked, sometimes in mid-sentence, so in a way, I am ideally suited, if you will pardon the pun, for this work. I'm like a double secret agent.

So, I just called and read all this to my cousin Dan to see what he thought, and he said that I sounded angry, but that it was okay because this is important stuff.

Funnily enough, though, I don't feel at all angry writing this. I just feel tired.

I just googled the definition of the word "diversity." The first thing that popped up was "the quality of being diverse or different; difference or unlikeness."

So if we aim for diversity, what we get are people who are defined by what they are not, what they are not like. We are included because of who we are not, because of who we are unlike.

I think it's well past time to change the language.

Because queer means so much more to me than just the absence of straightness.

Being trans is so much more complicated and nuanced for me than just not being a cisgender man or a woman. And for some trans people, being trans means that they do simply see themselves as a man, or a woman. I don't want to erase anyone because we share a word that means different things to each of us.

I want to flip the word "diversity" over and look at its underbelly. I want to start talking more about reality. I want to talk about what we are really talking about. I want to talk about what it costs marginalized voices when we step up to write or speak our truth to an audience that often does not include many faces or bodies that look like ours.

I write and speak about my experiences as a trans person. This by its very nature involves writing and speaking about things I was taught we are not to ever write or speak about: My body. My desires. My period. My body. Where I pee when out in public. My body. Where it fits. Where it belongs. How it doesn't.

So, this brings me to the story I want to tell you.

This last February I did a tour of small-town theatres in Alberta.

Rural Canada. Sort of by accident—it's a long story. I wasn't talking about trans issues, I wasn't supposed to be an activist; I was an artist, I was a storyteller, I was doing a show about my grandmother. The kind of show my agent thought he could sell to medium-sized theatres in small-town southern Alberta. And he was right, and so he did, and so there I was.

This tour had been block booked, they call it, which means that several municipal theatres all agree to bring an artist or show to the area to do the rounds, thus sharing the costs of travel and accommodations. Most of the theatregoers hold season's tickets, which means they go to every show the theatre presents, so they often see performances they might not have sought out, or artists they are not familiar with.

So, basically, I was a trans person telling family stories in small farming and resource towns to people who mostly had no idea I was trans. This is supposed to be what I dreamed of, right? But I wasn't invited to perform because nobody cared I was trans. It was because few of them knew I was trans. And that is a very different thing.

This is the part where you all study me and see if you even believe I could so-called pass as a man well enough for me to tell septuagenarian farmers and their wives stories about my dear departed grandmother for seventy-five minutes without them figuring out I wasn't exactly the clean-cut, granny-loving, nice young man they might have thought I was at first. Go ahead. Study my stubbleless cheekbones. Peruse the curve of my hips. Listen to the gilded timbre of my voice, and note my unusually long eyelashes. Observe the slender width of my wrists. It's okay. Really. I'm used to it.

I'm just going to stop here and read you a letter I received from an audience member who did figure me out:

Good morning, Ivan:
WOW!

What a performance last night. Let me say first that you are one great speaker. You touched me very deeply. I, too, am a storyteller; however, not in public. I have been told that I tell very good stories. For the most part, they are true stories, relating experiences I have had. And I think most people would think I am full of shit. Often, I wonder myself how all of this could be true.

Shortly before showtime I saw a post on Facebook indicating that a friend of mine had been given five tickets to the show, and she was looking for people that could use them. Being that I have always wanted to attend something at this theatre—I have never been before—not to mention the fact that I am attracted to this particular friend, I responded that I would love to go. She called me before the show and told me that the seats were not all together—damn, I would not get to sit with her. Then she told me that she had discovered that you were transgender (is that the right word?), and after some vacillating about attending, she decided she would go, and admitted that she had some prejudices about transgender people. I must admit that I am not sure where I stand about this either. However, how can I back out now? We did not sit together, but we spoke briefly as we entered the theatre after intermission, and she mentioned something about her reservations—I can't remember exactly what—and I jokingly told her that I might get kicked out. I said if that happens, just pretend you don't know me. She replied, "Too late, we have already been seen together in public."

Now to the point of my writing you. I have a couple of questions.

When you were talking about your grandma's heaven, and you said her heaven did not have a husband who beat his wife or fucked his children, were you referring to your grandfather, or perhaps your father? Or both, or neither?

What a bombshell that was, but I am sure you know that and intended it. I was shedding tears from that point on.

Here is the other question. Did you make eye contact with me several times during the course of the show? I was sitting in the front row slightly to your right of centre. I had the very distinct feeling that you did. And if so, do you do that with every person in the audience?

I went into the theatre with reservations, as I have said. And at first I was looking at you and thinking,

OK, he has the hips of a girl, no breasts, no whiskers, I
wonder if he has a penis? Anyway, it was not long until
all I saw was a loving, caring, brilliant human being.

 I felt compelled to share that with you.

 Have a great day,

 Darren, the Spiritual Redneck

Now. This is the part where some of you—and I know you mean
well, I truly do, and you are partly right—tell me that this is evidence
of progress, that this is a good thing. That Darren, the self-appointed
spiritual redneck, had his moment, that he learned something, and
that all of our hard work is paying off and we should feel happy. We
should feel grateful.

 And this is the part where I tell you how guilty I feel that I haven't
had the time or heart to write Darren back yet, and what kind of a
goddamned ambassador for all trans people everywhere am I that I
haven't been able to swallow everything this letter makes me feel and
write him a heartfelt and loving response thanking him for taking
the time to treat me like a human? Sort of.

 So, I guess part of what I'm saying is that part of taking care of
myself enough to do this work has lately involved acknowledging just
exactly what this work involves.

 Putting my body under the spotlight to be perused and pondered
and debated, even when I'm attempting to talk about something, about
anything, else. Pretending that as we engage in these debates—and we
have to, I know that, to keep from being disappeared, to fight for our

space and our rights and our dignity—I can be calm and reasonable while casually discussing whether or not I exist. All the while knowing that what may be armchair philosophy for some means actual life and death and liberty for trans people. Being polite and patient while knowing that my liberation is just someone else's learning opportunity.

And remembering that when I hear others—fat activists, feminists, black activists, Indigenous people, assault survivors, and people with disabilities—speak up, it is their bodies up there, too, their flesh and memories being questioned. And that the only way through is for us all to listen better.

I want to close by saying that I am truly, sincerely grateful for the opportunity to be here, so far away from home, and be offered a stage and a platform from which to speak to you all today. I'm truly glad that each and every one of you has chosen to be here with me. These are necessary and vital conversations, and I hope this one continues after we all leave this room in a few short minutes.

I'm humbled that I have been trusted by this festival, and all of you, to speak to these issues. And I want you to know, on my honour, I'm not angry. Well, not that angry. I'm hopeful and inspired and motivated and grateful. And really, really tired.

DEAR DARREN:

First of all, I want to thank you for overcoming your reservations about trans people enough to come to the theatre that night and listen to an actual trans person speak, even if, as you said, you really only showed up to see the venue, and maybe get closer to your friend. I met her after the show. She seemed nice. She bought my book and wanted to talk about aromatherapy and her homemade soap company. I would never have guessed she had prejudices about trans people.

It sounds like what happened for you is that you kind of accidentally saw my humanity, and I guess that is why I believe so deeply in the power of storytelling, why I am so viscerally certain that the simple act of one human listening to another is the only real way to foster compassion in an unknowing heart for someone who is different from them. Stories are the best tools I know.

I'm home now, sitting on my couch, full of homemade soup, with the little dog snoring beside me, stretched out against my leg like he does. It's been two years and nearly two months since you got up at 6:45 a.m. the day after my gig and wrote that email to me. My sincere apologies that it has taken me this long to respond. I guess I needed some time to think about it all before just reacting and firing off a response full of the feelings that your letter called up in me that morning. I'm glad I waited.

Before I address your questions, a little context: That was my first, and most likely last, tour of small-town southern Alberta. Bear with me while I tell you more than you probably ever wanted to know about how theatres book the shows in their season.

About a year before that tour, my booking agent talked me into flying to Edmonton with Jon, my guitar player, to do what they call a showcase. You get fifteen minutes to perform an excerpt of the show you are trying to pitch, to an audience made up mostly of artistic directors and volunteer board members of local theatres. The delegates then decide on a few productions they think they can sell to their season's ticket holders and theatre patrons, and if a handful of theatres all decide they like a certain performer or play, then they can do what the industry calls block book a show, and then several theatres all share the costs of bringing that production to their individual towns. My agent thought that the wholesome grandmother-story nature of that particular show would override the presenters' reluctance to book a show written and performed by a queer and trans person. That is not exactly how it went down.

What actually happened was the guy who introduced me at that showcase did not read the bio my agent sent ahead of time and instead, after a few words backstage before my set, made some assumptions and went out and introduced me as a nice young man from the Yukon who was going to tell a story about his grandmother. And so that is who the delegates saw and heard that day, and that is the show they thought they had booked. Just a nice young man telling stories about his grandmother.

The result was that I was on tour in small-town southern Alberta and some of my host theatres didn't even know that they had booked a trans performer. On the surface you could make an argument that this was a good thing, and that it shouldn't matter if I was trans or not, and you would sort of be right, in a perfect world.

But we both know that it is anything but a perfect world out there these days. Especially in Edson, Alberta, which the internet tells me is a town on the Yellowhead Highway with a population of a little over 8,000 people, most of whom work in the coal, oil, natural gas, and forestry industries. As I write this, your province just days ago elected by a landslide Jason Kenney of the United Conservative Party, who ran his team of racists and pipeline-loving Christians on a platform that also promised to roll back protections for LGBTQ youth in schools.

I'm not going to ask you who you voted for, Darren. I think that would be an invasive question.

I am going to ask you, though, to think about what it felt like for me to spend ten days on the road in small-town theatres where I often had no safe bathroom to use before I stepped out onto a stage in front of a full house of season's ticket holders, many of whom didn't know who I was or were unsure how they felt about me or harboured open prejudices about who I was.

I used the women's room at the theatre the previous night because I was wearing a silk pocket square and was afraid of getting punched out in the men's bathroom right before my show started. I knew the woman who ran the theatre in that town didn't know I was trans and had mistaken me for a young man because she kept saying in sound check that she didn't believe the part of my story about Scotch-taping over the square holes and recording cartoons over my aunt's Jane Fonda exercise videos because I was way too young to even know what a VHS even was. I didn't have the heart to tell her I was old enough to remember when everyone thought Betamax was going to be the next big thing.

I remember being very grateful that the theatre in Edson had a green room and a private bathroom. I remember my heart pounding every night of that tour until I locked my hotel room door behind me and flipped the door bolt to the safe position. The hotels I stayed in were mostly populated by oil rig workers and loggers, and at night I was nervous in the hallways and got the side-eye more than once from trios of dudes drinking beers out of coolers perched on tailgates in parking lots. In the mornings, I ignored the stares in the little breakfast rooms and ate my reconstituted scrambled eggs and yogurt cups and hoped that none of those coveralled, work-booted guys would pick a fight with me or Jon before we could finish our coffee and load up the gear and hit the highway. Jon's not a big guy, if you recall, and he's not used to being called a faggot like I am.

It kind of gave stage fright a whole new meaning for me, Darren, those shows did. Just a little context for you.

I drank more on that tour than I usually do, and I slept for a whole week when I got home.

Now to your questions. You asked me about when I was talking about my gran's heaven, and I said her heaven did not have a husband who beat his wife or fucked his children, and you wondered was I referring to my grandfather, or perhaps my father? Or both, or neither?

You said that line made you shed tears from that point on.

I can only assume that this line resonated somehow with your own history, Darren, and for that all I can offer you is my compassion and solidarity. I call this rattling someone's ghosts, and I know that line is difficult to hear. It's hard to say, even to this day, even alone to myself on the couch at home. I wrote that line not about my own father, who is a decent if complicated man. I didn't even write it about either of my grandfathers, really, neither of whom were particularly good or decent men. I wrote that line for all of the women in my family. I wrote that line to conjure up a heaven where all of us can one day be free of the fists and wrongful touch of anyone's father, anyone's grandfather. I wrote that line for your ghosts, too, Darren. I wrote that line for all of us.

Thank you for including the picture of yourself at the bottom of your email. I remember meeting you after the show, but I do not remember seeing you in the theatre. If you were sitting in the front row slightly to the right of centre, chances are it looked like I made eye contact with you. The truth is, when the lights are on my face like they need to be for you to see me up onstage, I can't really see too much of the audience. But I can feel you out there, and I can hear you, and believe me, I was listening. A good storyteller should always be listening.

Thanks for writing, Darren, and thank you for coming to my show, and for staying until the end. My hope is that my stories have done exactly what stories are meant to do, in their purest nature. I hope they made you see me, with girl hips, and beard-, breast-, and dickless, but full of my own truths. With my very human heart beating, just like yours.

Sincerely,

Ivan

11. CHEST

SHAME: A LOVE letter.

Do you remember all of your shame like I do? Does it creep into your chest when you wake up too early? Does it lie there, coiled beneath your scars?

Does it trickle down between the muscles of your back when you sweat inside the shirt you can't make yourself take off, even on the beach on your birthday? Born in August.

We walked along the powdery sand to find a place to put our towels, and I couldn't find any words to explain why I was crying on such a sunny day. Seven days later I can now say out loud that undressing in a crowd reveals what feels like a fading target on my chest, white semi circles where breast is now chest and round pink nipples I have not been able to feel for five years.

No one is staring at you, I tell myself. *There are all kinds of bodies here*, I tell myself.

But still. None that look like mine.

WHAT DID SHAME ever teach me, except to be ashamed?

I **HAVE A** lot of words for what I feel when I am the only trans person (that I know of) on the beach. In the gym. In the sauna change room bathroom doctor's office street or bedroom. "Dysphoria" is not one of them.

BE CAREFUL WHO is listening when you talk about your desires. Some people have poisonous ears.

I'M CHANGING MY stage name to Corinthian Leather. Wikipedia says it was often found in 1970s Chryslers, same as me.

Gender euphoria

Gender plethoria

Gender I'm boredia.

REASON NUMBER ELEVEN hundred and ninety-seven why I love the baritone saxophone so much is that it requires me to wear a chest harness. Requires.

PEOPLE LIKE TO make fun of people who take selfies. But some folks grow up feeling ugly. Maybe having control over their image, taking a picture that makes them feel beautiful or handsome or sexy, and posting it makes them feel better about how they look. Queers get called ugly. Butches do. Homophobia, transphobia, fatphobia, racism get aimed and fired at some of us. We are bombarded with images of who is allowed to be attractive and who is not. Maybe selfies are a way for some people to feel beautiful and get positive messages about their bodies. I know I always felt ugly when I was young, because I didn't know any handsome female-assigned people. I didn't know I was allowed to be attractive in any other way but pretty. I also know I still carry some of that feeling ugly around with me to this day.

ONE DAY I hope to tell a true story about a very old trans person. I want it to be a long and kind of boring story where the only pain is in my ancient bones and the biggest struggle of my day is how I'm going to get the gravy boat down from that weird little cupboard above the fridge because I'm having a giant dinner party and the family is coming over. We will eat dinner and then push the plates aside and one of the kids will say, "Tell us a story."

And so I will.

ACKNOWLEDGMENTS

I would like to thank Arsenal Pulp Press for their unflinching and ongoing support. I am ever grateful to Brian Lam, Robert Ballantyne, Oliver McPartlin, Shirarose Wilensky, and the always fabulous Cynara Geissler for their hard work and for publishing the kind of books my heart needs to read.

I need to acknowledge the support of the Canada Council for the Arts and the BC Arts Council, and the English Department at Simon Fraser University for the space and time to create.

My undying respect and love to Bet Cecil, Mary Bryson, Jack Barker, Janine Fuller, Kate Bornstein, and the late Jim Deva. May my words bring you a fraction of the love and honour knowing you has brought to me.

Photo by Emily Cooper

IVAN COYOTE is the award-winning author, co-author, or co-editor of eleven other books, including *Tomboy Survival Guide*, shortlisted for the Hilary Weston Writers' Trust Nonfiction Prize and an American Library Association Stonewall Honor Book. They are also the creator of four short films, as well as three CDs that combine storytelling with music. Ivan is a seasoned stage performer and an audience favourite at storytelling, literary, film, and folk music festivals. Ivan shares their time between Vancouver, BC, and Whitehorse, Yukon.

ivancoyote.com